25/9/20

D0590785

The Delia Collection
Puddings

BBC
BOOKS

Published by BBC Books
BBC Worldwide Ltd
Woodlands
80 Wood Lane
London W12 OTT

First published in 2006
Reprinted 2006, 2007

Text © Delia Smith 2006
The moral right of the author has been asserted
Design © New Crane Ltd 2006

A proportion of these recipes has been published
previously in *Delia's Complete Illustrated Cookery
Course, Delia Smith's Winter Collection, Delia
Smith's Summer Collection, Delia's How To Cook
Books One, Two* and *Three, Delia Smith's Christmas,
Delia's Vegetarian Collection, Delia's Christmas Easy*
magazine and *Delia's Complete Christmas* magazine.

All rights reserved. No part of this book may be
reproduced, stored in a retrieval system or transmitted
in any form or by any means, including electronic,
electrostatic, magnetic tape, mechanical, photocopying,
recording or otherwise without prior permission in
writing from the copyright holder and publisher.

Edited for BBC Worldwide Ltd
by New Crane Ltd

Editor: Sarah Randell
Designer: Paul Webster
Sub-editors: Heather Cupit, Diana Galligan
Recipe Testing: Pauline Curran
Commissioning Editor for the BBC: Vivien Bowler

ISBN 978 0 563 49343 3

Printed and bound in Singapore
Colour separation
by Butler & Tanner

Cover photograph: Peter Knab
Title page photograph: Michael Paul
For further photographic credits, see page 136

Introduction

When I look back over my years of cookery writing, I have to admit that very often, decisions about what to do have sprung from what my own particular needs are. As a very busy person who has to work, run a home and cook, I felt it was extremely useful to have, for instance, summer recipes in one book – likewise winter and Christmas, giving easy access to those specific seasons.

This, my latest venture, has come about for similar reasons. Thirty six years of recipe writing have produced literally thousands of recipes. So I now feel what would be really helpful is to create a kind of ordered library (so I don't have to rack my brains and wonder which book this or that recipe is in!). Thus, if I want to make a pudding, I don't have to look through the pudding sections of various books, but have the whole lot in one convenient collection.

In compiling these collections, I have chosen what I think are the best and most popular recipes and, at the same time, have added some that are completely new. It is my hope that those who have not previously tried my recipes will now have smaller collections to sample, and that those dedicated followers will appreciate an ordered library to provide easy access and a reminder of what has gone before and may have been forgotten.

Delia Smith

Conversion Tables

All these are approximate conversions, which have either been rounded up or down. In a few recipes it has been necessary to modify them very slightly. Never mix metric and imperial measures in one recipe, stick to one system or the other.

All spoon measurements used throughout this book are level unless specified otherwise.

All butter is salted unless specified otherwise.

All recipes have been double-tested, using a standard convection oven. If you are using a fan oven, adjust the cooking temperature according to the manufacturer's handbook.

Weights	
½ oz	10 g
¾	20
1	25
1½	40
2	50
2½	60
3	75
4	110
4½	125
5	150
6	175
7	200
8	225
9	250
10	275
12	350
1 lb	450
1 lb 8 oz	700
2	900
3	1.35 kg

Volume	
2 fl oz	55 ml
3	75
5 (¼ pint)	150
10 (½ pint)	275
1 pint	570
1¼	725
1¾	1 litre
2	1.2
2½	1.5
4	2.25

Dimensions	
⅛ inch	3 mm
¼	5
½	1 cm
¾	2
1	2.5
1¼	3
1½	4
1¾	4.5
2	5
2½	6
3	7.5
3½	9
4	10
5	13
5¼	13.5
6	15
6½	16
7	18
7½	19
8	20
9	23
9½	24
10	25.5
11	28
12	30

Oven temperatures		
Gas mark 1	275°F	140°C
2	300	150
3	325	170
4	350	180
5	375	190
6	400	200
7	425	220
8	450	230
9	475	240

Contents

Pies
Crumbles
Cobblers

Apple and Almond Crumble
Serves 6-8

For the filling

1 lb 8 oz (700 g) Bramley cooking apples

8 oz (225 g) Cox's apples

1 oz (25 g) light brown soft sugar

1 teaspoon ground cinnamon

1 teaspoon ground cloves

For the crumble

4 oz (110 g) whole almonds (with skins left on)

3 oz (75 g) chilled butter, cut into small dice

6 oz (175 g) self-raising flour, sifted

2 teaspoons ground cinnamon

4 oz (110 g) demerara sugar

You will also need either an oval ovenproof baking dish, 7½ x 11 inches (19 x 28 cm), 1¾ inches (4.5 cm) deep, or a round ovenproof baking dish with a diameter of 9½ inches (24 cm), 1¾ inches (4.5 cm) deep.

Pre-heat the oven to gas mark 6, 400°F (200°C).

This is a moveable feast because absolutely any fruit can be used. I love it with peaches or apricots in summer, in spring it's good with rhubarb (use 2 lb/900 g fruit and 2 oz/50 g sugar to sweeten), and in autumn I use half blackberries and half apples. Whatever fruit you use, though, the great thing about the topping is that it bakes to a lovely short, crumbly crispness that is almost crunchy.

Begin by preparing the apples. I always find the best way to do this is to cut them first in quarters, then pare off the peel with a potato peeler and slice out the cores. Now cut them into thickish slices and toss them in a bowl with the sugar, cinnamon and ground cloves, then place them in the baking dish and put to one side.

Next, make the crumble, which couldn't be simpler, as it is all made in a processor. All you do is place the butter, sifted flour, cinnamon and sugar in the processor and give it a whiz till it resembles crumbs. Next, add the almonds and process again, not too fast, until they are fairly finely chopped and there are still a few chunky bits. If you don't have a processor, in a large bowl, rub the butter into the sifted flour until it resembles crumbs, then stir in the cinnamon, sugar and almonds, which should be fairly finely chopped by hand. Now simply sprinkle the crumble mixture all over the apples, spreading it right up to the edges of the dish, and, using the flat of your hands, press it down quite firmly all over; the more tightly it is packed together the crisper it will be. Then finish off by lightly running a fork all over the surface.

Now bake the crumble on the centre shelf of the oven for 35-40 minutes, by which time the apples will be soft and the topping golden brown and crisp. Leave it to rest for 10-15 minutes before serving, then serve it warm with custard or pouring cream.

Pile-it-high Orange and Rhubarb Meringue Pie
Serves 6-8

For the pastry

1½ oz (40 g) softened butter, cut into smallish lumps

1½ oz (40 g) softened pure lard, cut into smallish lumps

6 oz (175 g) plain flour, plus a little extra for rolling out

For the filling

1 lb 8 oz (700 g) rhubarb

grated zest and juice of 3 oranges

3 oz (75 g) golden caster sugar

3 large egg yolks

3 tablespoons cornflour

For the meringue

3 large egg whites (minimum)

6 oz (175 g) golden caster sugar

or you can use as many egg whites as you have:

4 egg whites need 8 oz (225 g) sugar, 5 need 10 oz (275 g) sugar, 6 need 12 oz (350 g) sugar

You will also need a 9 inch (23 cm) tart tin, 1¼ inches (3 cm) deep, lightly greased, and a solid baking sheet.

Pre-heat the oven to gas mark 5, 375°F (190°C), and pre-heat the baking sheet as well.

The flavour of orange zest does something quite magical to the flavour of rhubarb, and this light, fluffy meringue pie is a perfect dessert for late spring. 'Pile-it-high meringue', incidentally, applies only if you have extra egg whites to use up or *want* to make the meringue high. If not, you can simply use the egg whites in the recipe: it will still be superb!

Begin by making the pastry: rub the fats into the flour and add enough cold water to make a smooth dough that leaves the bowl clean. Then wrap it in a polythene bag and leave it in the fridge for 30 minutes to rest and become more elastic. Meanwhile, wash and trim the rhubarb and cut it into chunks, place in a shallow baking dish and sprinkle in the grated orange zest, followed by the sugar.

Take the pastry from the fridge, roll it out to a round on a lightly floured surface (giving it quarter-turns as you do so) and use it to line the tin, pressing it up a little way above the edge of the tin. Next, prick the base all over with a fork and use some of the egg yolks to paint all over the base and sides to provide a seal. Put the tin on the pre-heated baking sheet on a high shelf in the oven and place the rhubarb on the lowest shelf. The pastry should take about 20-25 minutes to brown and crisp, and the rhubarb about 25-30 minutes to become soft. Then remove them from the oven.

While you're waiting for that, you can pour the orange juice into a small saucepan. Use a little of it to mix the cornflour to a smooth paste in a bowl, then bring the rest up to simmering point. Next, pour the hot orange juice on to the cornflour mixture and pour the whole lot back into the saucepan. Whisk over the heat with a small balloon whisk till it becomes very thick indeed, then remove it from the heat.

Now strain the cooked rhubarb over a bowl, then add the rhubarb juices and the remaining egg yolks to the cornflour mixture and, still whisking, bring it up to the boil again. Remove from the heat, tip the strained rhubarb into the bowl and stir the cornflour mixture into it.

Now, for the meringue, put the egg whites into a large, roomy, clean bowl and, using an electric hand whisk, beat them until they reach the stage where, when you lift the whisk, little peaks stand up and just slightly turn over. Next, beat the sugar in, 1 tablespoon at a time, whisking well after each addition. Pour the rhubarb mixture into the pastry shell, then spoon the meringue mixture over, making sure that it covers the edges of the pastry with no gaps. Then just pile it on, 'normal', high or very high.

Place the pie on the centre shelf of the oven, at the same temperature as before, and bake it for 25 minutes or until the outside of the meringue is golden. Remove it from the oven and leave for about 2 hours before serving.

Key Lime Pie
Serves 8-10

For the base

3½ oz (95 g) butter

6 oz (175 g) digestive biscuits

2 oz (50 g) Grape-Nuts breakfast cereal

For the filling

1 tablespoon grated lime zest (zest of 3 limes)

5 fl oz (150 ml) lime juice (juice of 4-5 large limes)

3 large egg yolks

1 x 397 g tin condensed milk

To finish

a little crème fraîche

thin lime slices

You will also need a loose-based fluted tart tin with a diameter of 9 inches (23 cm), 1 inch (2.5 cm) deep, and a solid baking sheet.

Pre-heat the oven to gas mark 4, 350°F (180°C).

This is a very famous recipe from Florida, where a certain special variety of limes called Key limes are used. Their season is short and there aren't enough grown to export; however, the pie tastes just as good with other varieties of lime in this authentic American recipe.

Traditional Key lime pie has always had a crumb crust, and I have discovered that the addition of Grape-Nuts breakfast cereal gives the whole thing extra crunch. So begin by placing the butter in a pan over the lowest heat to melt, then crush the digestive biscuits. The easiest way to do this is to lay them out flat in a polythene bag and crush them with a rolling pin, rolling over using a lot of pressure. Now empty the contents of the bag into a bowl and mix in the Grape-Nuts, then add the melted butter and mix well.

Next, place the butter-crumb mixture in the flan tin and, using your hands, press it down evenly and firmly all over the base and up the sides of the tin. Then place it on the baking sheet and bake on the centre shelf of the oven for 10-12 minutes, or until crisp and golden brown.

While that's happening, place the egg yolks and lime zest in a bowl and, using an electric hand mixer, whisk them for about 2 minutes, or until the egg has thickened, then add the condensed milk and whisk for another 4 minutes. Finally, add the lime juice and give it another quick whisk, then pour the whole lot on to the baked crust and return it to the oven for another 20 minutes, or until it feels just set when you lightly press the centre with your little finger. Now remove it from the oven and, when it's completely cold, cover it with clingfilm and chill until needed. Serve cut in slices with crème fraîche and a twist of lime for decoration.

A Very Easy One-crust Gooseberry Pie
Serves 6

For the pastry

6 oz (175 g) plain flour, plus a little extra for rolling out

1½ oz (40 g) softened pure lard, cut into smallish lumps

1½ oz (40 g) softened butter, cut into smallish lumps

1 small egg yolk

2 rounded tablespoons semolina

For the filling

1 lb 8 oz (700 g) gooseberries, topped and tailed

3 oz (75 g) golden caster sugar

For the glaze

1 small egg white

6 sugar cubes, crushed

You will also need a solid baking sheet, lightly greased.

This American idea for making a pie is blissfully easy – no baking tins and no lids to be cut, fitted and fluted. It looks very attractive because you can see the fruit inside and, because there is less pastry, it's a little easier on the waistline.

Make up the pastry by sifting the flour into a large mixing bowl, then rubbing the fats into it lightly with your fingertips, lifting everything up and letting it fall back into the bowl to give it a good airing. When the mixture reaches the crumb stage, sprinkle in enough cold water to bring it together to a smooth dough that leaves the bowl absolutely clean, with no crumbs left. Give it a little light knead to bring it fully together, then place the pastry in a polythene bag in the fridge for 30 minutes.

After that, pre-heat the oven to gas mark 6, 400°F (200°C). Then roll the pastry out on a lightly floured flat surface to a round of approximately 14 inches (35.5 cm) – as you roll, give it quarter-turns so that it ends up as round as you can make it (don't worry, though, about ragged edges: they're fine). Now carefully roll the pastry round the rolling pin and transfer it to the centre of the lightly greased baking sheet.

To prevent the pastry getting soggy from any excess juice, paint the base with egg yolk (you'll need to cover approximately a 10 inch/25.5 cm circle in the centre), then sprinkle the semolina lightly over this. The semolina is there to absorb the juices and the egg provides a waterproof coating.

Now simply pile the gooseberries in the centre of the pastry, sprinkling them with sugar as you go. Then all you do is turn in the edges of the pastry: if any breaks, just patch it back on again – it's all meant to be ragged and interesting. Brush the pastry surface all round with the egg white, then crush the sugar cubes with a rolling pin and sprinkle over the pastry (the idea of using crushed cubes is to get a less uniform look than you would with granulated). Now pop the pie on to the highest shelf of the oven and bake for approximately 35 minutes or until the crust is golden brown. Remove from the oven and serve warm with chilled crème fraîche or ice cream.

VARIATIONS

Rhubarb Use 1 lb 8 oz (700 g) rhubarb and 3 oz (75 g) sugar to sweeten, or try one of the following variations on the plain fruit filling: add the grated zest of 2 oranges or 1 rounded teaspoon grated fresh ginger (or powdered ginger) and soft brown sugar.

Blackcurrants Use 1 lb 8 oz (700 g) blackcurrants and 2 oz (50 g) sugar to sweeten.

Blackberry and apple Use 1 lb (450 g) apples, 8 oz (225 g) blackberries and 2 oz (50 g) sugar to sweeten.

Cherries Use a hazelnut pastry made with 6 oz (175 g) plain flour, 2 oz (50 g) ground hazelnuts, ¼ teaspoon ground cinnamon and fats as for the gooseberry pie. Use 1 lb 8 oz (700 g) cherries, stoned, and only 1½ oz (40 g) sugar to sweeten the fruit.

Apricots Use hazelnut pastry, as above, with 1 lb 8 oz (700 g) apricots, stoned and quartered, plus 1 oz (25 g) toasted slivered almonds.

Raspberries and redcurrants Use hazelnut pastry, as above, with 1 lb 4 oz (570 g) raspberries, 4 oz (110 g) redcurrants and 2 oz (50 g) sugar to sweeten.

Plums Use hazelnut pastry, as above, with 1 lb 8 oz (700 g) plums, stoned and quartered, and 2 oz (50 g) sugar to sweeten.

Plum and Almond Buttermilk Cobbler
Serves 6

For the filling

2 lb 8 oz (1.15 kg) medium plums

2 oz (50 g) golden caster sugar

For the topping

2 tablespoons flaked almonds

6 fl oz (175 ml) buttermilk

8 oz (225 g) plain flour, sifted

½ teaspoon salt

3 teaspoons baking powder

1 teaspoon ground cinnamon

4 oz (110 g) ice-cold butter,
cut into pieces

1 tablespoon demerara sugar,
mixed with 1 teaspoon ground
cinnamon

You will also need a baking dish
about 9 inches (23 cm) in diameter,
2 inches (5 cm) deep.

Pre-heat the oven to gas mark 7,
425°F (220°C).

I have a small Victoria plum tree, but so laden is it every year that Richard, who helps us with our garden, has to put a stake under one of the branches. This is one of our favourite family puddings, which allows the plums to cook in their own luscious juice and provides a cloud of crisp fluffy topping. Damsons are a lovely alternative (you may need a little extra sugar). Either way, serve it with some chilled Jersey cream or vanilla ice cream.

To prepare the plums, slide the tip of a sharp knife, following the natural line of the fruit, all around each plum through to the stone. Then, using both hands, give it a twist and divide it in half. Remove the stone and cut each plum into quarters. Now all you do is arrange the fruit in the baking dish, scattering the caster sugar as you go.

To make the topping, place the sifted flour, salt, baking powder, cinnamon and butter into the bowl of a food processor. Then switch on and give it a pulse (on/off) action several times until the mixture resembles fine breadcrumbs. Then pour in the buttermilk and switch on again briefly until you have a thick, very sticky dough. Now spoon tablespoons of the mixture over the fruit in rocky mounds – the more haphazardly you do this, the better.

Lastly, sprinkle the sugar and cinnamon all over, followed by the flaked almonds, then pop the dish on to a high shelf in the oven for 30 minutes or until it is a crusty golden brown. Serve the cobbler warm from the oven.

Traditional Apple Pie with a Cheddar Crust and Traditional English Custard
Serves 8

For the pastry

3 oz (75 g) mild Cheddar, coarsely grated

8 oz (225 g) plain flour, plus a little extra for rolling out

2 oz (50 g) softened butter

2 oz (50 g) softened pure lard

For the filling

2 lb (900 g) Bramley cooking apples

2 lb (900 g) Cox's apples

1 tablespoon fine semolina

3 oz (75 g) golden caster sugar

12 whole cloves

1 large egg, beaten, to glaze

For the custard

1 vanilla pod

1½ pints (850 ml) double cream

9 large egg yolks

1½ dessertspoons cornflour

3 oz (75 g) golden caster sugar

You will also need a rimmed metal pie dish, 9 inches (23 cm) in diameter and 1¼ inches (3 cm) deep with sloping sides, and a solid baking sheet.

This is a huge family apple pie, which I often call 'More Apple Than Pie', as it has four pounds of apples in it. Putting Cheddar in the crust gives it a lovely crisp, flaky texture without a strong cheese flavour. I offer custard here as it has been made down the centuries – with thick double cream – but you can, if you wish, modify this extravagance by using single cream or creamy whole milk.

First, make the pastry. Sift the flour into a roomy bowl, holding the sieve up high to give it a good airing, then add the butter and lard cut into small pieces, rubbing the fats into the flour with your fingertips until it reaches the crumbly stage. Now add the grated Cheddar and enough cold water to make a soft dough that leaves the bowl clean (about 3 tablespoons). Then turn it out on to a board, knead it briefly and lightly, then pop it into a polythene bag and leave it to rest in the fridge for about 30 minutes.

Meanwhile, peel, quarter and core the apples and then cut them into very thin slices straight into a bowl, mixing the 2 varieties together. Pre-heat the oven to gas mark 7, 425°F (220°C). Next, take a little less than half of the pastry and roll it out very thinly on a lightly floured surface to about 12 inches (30 cm) in diameter, to line the base and sides of the pie dish. Trim the edges and leave unused pastry aside for the trimmings. Then scatter the semolina over the base of the pastry and after that pile in the apple slices, building up the layers closely and scattering in the sugar and cloves as you go. Then press and pack the apples tightly. Now roll the remaining pastry out, again very thinly, to make the lid, this time 16 inches (40 cm) in diameter. Brush the rim of the pastry base with a little of the beaten egg and carefully lift the lid over the top. Press the edges together to get a good seal all round, then trim, using a knife. Finally, gather up the trimmings and re-roll them to cut out into leaf shapes. Brush the surface of the pie with beaten egg, make a small hole in the centre the size of a 10p piece (to allow the steam to escape) and arrange the leaves on top. Now, with the back of a small knife, 'knock up' the edges, then flute them, using your thumb and the back of the knife. Now brush the whole lot with beaten egg, then place the pie on the baking sheet and bake on a high shelf for 10 minutes. After that, reduce the temperature to gas mark 5, 375°F (190°C) and cook for a further

45 minutes or until it has turned a deep golden brown. Then remove the pie from the oven and allow it to stand for at least 20 minutes before serving with the custard.

To make the custard, begin by splitting the vanilla pod lengthways and using the end of a teaspoon to scoop out the seeds. Then place the pod and the seeds in a saucepan, along with the cream. Now place the pan over a gentle heat and heat it to just below simmering point. While the cream is heating, whisk the egg yolks, cornflour and sugar together in a medium bowl, using a balloon whisk. Next, remove the vanilla pod from the hot cream. Then, whisking the egg mixture all the time with one hand, gradually pour the hot cream into the bowl. When it's all in, immediately return the whole lot back to the saucepan, using a rubber spatula. Now back it goes on to the same gentle heat as you continue whisking, until the custard is thick and smooth, which will happen as soon as it reaches simmering point. (If you do overheat it and it looks grainy, don't worry, just transfer it to a bowl and continue to whisk until it becomes smooth again.) Pour the custard into a jug and serve with the pie. If you want to make the custard in advance, pour it into a bowl, cover the surface with clingfilm and leave to cool. Then, to serve it warm later, remove the clingfilm, and sit the bowl over a pan of barely simmering water.

Traditional Apple Pie
with a Cheddar Crust

Traditional Lemon Meringue Pie
Serves 6

For the pastry

4 oz (110 g) plain flour, plus a little extra for rolling out

a pinch of salt

1 oz (25 g) softened butter, cut into smallish lumps

1 oz (25 g) softened pure lard, cut into smallish lumps

For the filling

grated zest and juice of 2 large lemons

3 tablespoons cornflour

2 oz (50 g) golden caster sugar

3 large egg yolks

1½ oz (40 g) butter

For the meringue

3 large egg whites

6 oz (175 g) golden caster sugar

You will also need a 1½ inch (4 cm) deep, sloping-sided, non-stick pie tin with a ½ inch (1 cm) rim, a base diameter of 7 inches (18 cm) and a top diameter of 9½ inches (24 cm), and a solid baking sheet.

Everyone on my cookery team agreed that this famous English classic needed a revival. It is supremely light, squashy and fragrant with lemons. How did we ever forget about it?

Start by making the pastry. First, sift the flour and pinch of salt into a large bowl, holding the sieve up high to give the flour a good airing. Then add the butter and lard and, using only your fingertips, lightly rub the fats into the flour, again lifting the mixture up high. When everything is crumbly, sprinkle in 1 tablespoon of water. Start to mix the pastry with a flat-bladed knife and then finish off with your hands, adding a few more drops of water, until you have a smooth dough that will leave the bowl clean. Then pop the pastry into a polythene bag and let it rest in the fridge for 30 minutes. Pre-heat the oven to gas mark 5, 375°F (190°C) and put the baking sheet in to pre-heat at the same time.

Next, transfer the pastry to a flat, lightly floured surface and roll it out to a circle about ½ inch (1 cm) larger all round than the rim of the tin. Cut a ½ inch (1 cm) strip from the edge of the pastry, dampen the rim of the tin with water and fix the strip round it, pressing down well. Dampen the strip before lining the tin with the pastry circle, making sure you don't trap any air underneath it. Then prick the base all over with a fork. Place the tin on the baking sheet and bake on a high shelf in the pre-heated oven for 20-25 minutes, or until cooked through. After that, remove the pastry case from the oven, and immediately lower the heat to gas mark 2, 300°F (150°C) for the meringue.

Meanwhile, make the filling. Measure 10 fl oz (275 ml) water into a jug, and spoon the cornflour and sugar into a bowl. Add enough of the water to mix the cornflour to a smooth paste, then pour the rest of the water, along with the grated lemon zest, into a small saucepan. Bring this up to the boil, then pour it gradually on to the cornflour, mixing all the time until it's smooth.

Now return the mixture to the saucepan and bring it back to the boil, still mixing. Next, simmer very gently for about a minute, stirring all the time to prevent it from catching. Then remove the pan from the heat and beat in the egg yolks, lemon juice and lastly, the butter. Now pour the lemon mixture into the pastry case.

Finally, for the meringue, use a large, spanking clean, grease-free bowl and in it whisk the egg whites until they form stiff peaks. Now beat in a quarter of the sugar at a time until it is all incorporated, then spoon the meringue on top of the pie, taking it to the very edge of the pastry rim with a palette knife, so it seals the edge completely. (With your knife you can also make a few decorative swirls.) Bake in the oven on the centre shelf for 45 minutes, by which time the meringue will have turned pale beige, and be crisp on the outside and squashy within. Serve warm or cold, but if warm, leave it to settle for about 20 minutes. Chilled pouring cream is a nice accompaniment.

English Gooseberry Cobbler
Serves 6

For the filling

2 lb (900 g) young green
gooseberries, topped and tailed

4 oz (110 g) golden caster sugar

2 tablespoons elderflower cordial

For the topping

8 oz (225 g) plain flour, sifted

½ teaspoon salt

3 teaspoons baking powder

4 oz (110 g) ice-cold butter,
cut into pieces

6 fl oz (175 ml) milk

6 demerara sugar cubes, crushed
coarsely, or 1 heaped teaspoon
loose sugar

You will also need a baking dish,
about 9 inches (23 cm) in diameter,
and 2½ inches (6 cm) deep.

Pre-heat the oven to gas mark 7,
425°F (220°C).

This is a classic English version of a fruit cobbler, but speeded up with the aid of a food processor – which makes it one of the fastest baked fruit desserts imaginable.

All you do is arrange the fruit, caster sugar and elderflower cordial in the baking dish, then get on with the topping. Place the sifted flour, salt, baking powder and butter into a food processor. Then switch on and pulse it several times until the mixture resembles fine breadcrumbs. Next, pour in the milk and switch on again briefly until you have a thick, very sticky dough.

Now spoon tablespoons of the mixture over the fruit – the more haphazardly you do this, the better. Lastly, sprinkle the crushed sugar over the top of the dough, then pop the dish on to a high shelf in the oven for 25-30 minutes or until it is a crusty golden brown. Serve it warm from the oven with ice cream.

VARIATIONS

Rhubarb Use 2 lb (900 g) rhubarb and add the grated zest of an orange to the fruit, and the grated zest of ½ orange to the dough. Use the same quantity of sugar to sweeten the fruit.

Mixed fruit Use 2 lb (900 g) mixed fruit – peaches, apricots, plums, raspberries – with 2 oz (50 g) sugar to sweeten.

Pumpkin Pie
Serves 8

For the pastry

1½ oz (40 g) pecan nuts

6 oz (175 g) plain flour, plus a little extra for rolling out

½ oz (10 g) icing sugar

a pinch of salt

3 oz (75 g) softened butter

1 large egg yolk

For the filling

1 lb (450 g) prepared weight pumpkin flesh, cut into 1 inch (2.5 cm) chunks

2 large eggs, plus 1 large yolk (reserve the white)

1 tablespoon molasses

3 oz (75 g) dark brown soft sugar

1 teaspoon ground cinnamon

½ teaspoon freshly grated nutmeg

½ teaspoon ground allspice

½ teaspoon ground cloves

½ teaspoon ground ginger

10 fl oz (275 ml) double cream

You will also need a 9 inch (23 cm) diameter, loose-based, fluted tart tin, 1½ inches (4 cm) deep, lightly greased, and a solid baking sheet.

Pre-heat the oven to gas mark 4, 350°F (180°C).

This recipe uses a version of shortcrust pastry that is used for sweet open-faced flans and tarts. It's richer than shortcrust, but very crisp, and the eggs give it a shortbread quality. Nuts can sometimes be added; here there are toasted pecans, although walnuts or hazelnuts can be used, or the pastry can be made without nuts if you prefer. In autumn, I love the velvet texture of pumpkin, but this tart could be made with butternut squash.

To begin this you need to toast the pecan nuts. First of all, when the oven has pre-heated, spread the nuts out on the baking sheet and toast them lightly for 6-8 minutes, using a timer so that you don't forget them. After that, remove them from the oven to a chopping board (turning the oven off for now) and let them cool a little. Then either chop them really finely by hand or in a processor, using the pulse action. Be careful here, though, because if you overdo it they will go oily.

For the pastry, first of all sift the flour, icing sugar and the pinch of salt into a large bowl, holding the sieve up high to give it a good airing. Then add the butter and start cutting it into the flour using a knife, then, using only your fingertips, lightly and gently rub it into the flour, again lifting the mixture up high all the time to give it a good airing. When everything is crumbly, add the chopped nuts, then sprinkle in about 1 tablespoon of water and the egg yolk. Start to mix the pastry with a knife and then finish off with your hands, lightly bringing it together (you may need to add more water) until you have a smooth dough that will leave the bowl clean. Then pop it into a polythene bag and let it rest in the fridge for 30 minutes. Meanwhile, pre-heat the oven to gas mark 4, 350°F (180°C) with the baking sheet inside. Now place a steamer over a pan of simmering water, add the pumpkin, put a lid on and steam for 15-20 minutes until the pieces feel tender when tested with a skewer. After that, place a large, coarse sieve over a bowl and press the pumpkin through it to extract any seeds or fibres. By this time the pastry will have rested, so now remove it from the fridge. Roll it out into a circle on a surface lightly dusted with flour, and as you roll, give it quarter-turns to keep the round shape. Roll it into a circle about 12 inches (30 cm) in diameter, as thinly as possible. Now transfer it, rolling it over the pin, to the tin. Press lightly and firmly all over the base and sides of the tin, easing any overlapping pastry back down the sides, as it is important not to stretch this bit too much. Now trim the edge, leaving ¼ inch (5 mm) above the rim of the tin all round. Then prick the base all over with a fork and brush it and the sides with the reserved egg white, lightly beaten. Now place the tin on the pre-heated baking sheet on the centre shelf of the oven and bake it for 20-25 minutes, until the pastry is crisp and golden. Check halfway through the cooking time to make sure that the pastry isn't rising up in the centre. If it is, just prick it again a couple of times and press it back down again with your hands.

Now for the filling. First, lightly whisk the eggs and extra yolk together in a large bowl. Next, measure the molasses (lightly greasing the spoon first, as this makes things easier), then just push the molasses off the spoon with a rubber spatula into a saucepan. Add the sugar, spices and the cream, then bring it up to simmering point, giving it a whisk to mix everything together. Then pour it over the eggs and whisk it again briefly. Now add the pumpkin purée, still whisking to combine everything thoroughly, then pour the filling into a jug. When the pastry case is ready, remove it from the oven on the baking sheet, using an oven glove. Then pour half the filling in, return it to the oven and, with the shelf half out, pour in the rest of the filling and slide the shelf back in. Bake the pie for 35-40 minutes, by which time it will puff up round the edges but still feel slightly wobbly in the centre. Then remove it from the oven and place the tin on a wire cooling rack. I prefer to serve this chilled (stored, loosely covered in foil, in the fridge) with some equally chilled crème fraîche, but warm or at room temperature would be fine. In America, ice cream is the preferred accompaniment.

Mincemeat and Apple Jalousie
Serves 8

14 oz (400 g) mincemeat

1 small Bramley cooking apple
(8 oz/225 g)

zest of 1 orange

½ teaspoon ground mixed spice

2 tablespoons rum

1 x 375 g pack fresh ready-rolled
puff pastry

a little plain flour for dusting

1 large egg, lightly beaten

1 dessertspoon golden granulated
sugar mixed with ¼ teaspoon
ground cinnamon

1 tablespoon sifted icing sugar

You will also need a large, solid
baking tray, lightly greased.

All you need here is some mincemeat, a Bramley apple and some ready-rolled puff pastry, and from there on it's all plain sailing. At Christmas time, this can be cut into 16 small squares as an alternative to mince pies. The jalousie freezes well – I freeze it raw and defrost it before glazing, sprinkling with sugar and cinnamon, and baking.

First of all, put the mincemeat into a large bowl, then quarter the apple, cut away the core and chop it fairly small with the skin on (this can be done in a processor using the pulse button). Next, mix the apple, orange zest, spice and rum together with the mincemeat, and give it all a good stir. Pre-heat the oven to gas mark 6, 400°F (200°C).

Now unroll the pastry on to a surface, lightly dusted with flour, and roll it slightly thinner so it measures 12 x 18 inches (30 x 45 cm). After that, cut it into 2 long rectangles, which measure 6 x 18 inches (15 x 45 cm) each. Take 1 rectangle of pastry, roll it a little thinner and bigger, then fold it in half lengthways and, with a sharp knife, cut diagonally about 2 inches (5 cm) into the fold at 1 inch (2.5 cm) intervals all along. Next, place the second rectangle of pastry on the baking tray and pile the mincemeat filling on to the pastry, leaving a 1 inch (2.5 cm) border all round, and brush that border with a little cold water.

Now unfold the first rectangle of pastry and place it over the mincemeat and, using your thumbs, press the edges all around the filling to seal them. Finally, trim the pastry to ½ inch (1 cm) around the filling and use a small knife to crimp the edges. Brush the jalousie all over with the beaten egg and then sprinkle the sugar and cinnamon mixture over the top. Bake for 30-35 minutes and sprinkle with the icing sugar just before serving with cream, custard or, at Christmas time, it is particularly nice with rum butter.

Raspberry Crumble
Serves 6

For the filling

1 lb 2 oz (500 g) raspberries

1 tablespoon golden caster sugar

For the crumble topping

8 oz (225 g) plain flour, sifted

4 oz (110 g) butter, at room temperature, cut into small pieces

3 oz (75 g) light brown soft sugar

You will also need a round, shallow ovenproof baking dish with a diameter of 9 inches (23 cm), 1½ inches (4 cm) deep.

Pre-heat the oven to gas mark 4, 350°F (180°C).

I think this particular crumble is nicest baked in a shallow fluted ceramic dish (or something similar). This is a lovely crumble for the summer months.

First, make the topping. All you do is place the sifted flour, butter and sugar in the processor and give it a whiz until it resembles crumbs. If you don't have a processor, place the flour in a large mixing bowl, then add the butter and rub it into the flour lightly, using your fingertips. Then when it all looks crumbly, and the fat has been dispersed fairly evenly, add the sugar and combine that well with the rest.

Now arrange the raspberries in the dish and sprinkle over the sugar, then the crumble mixture, spreading it out all over the fruit with a fork. Place the crumble on a high shelf in the oven and bake it for 40 minutes until the top is golden. Serve with chilled pouring cream or vanilla ice cream.

Apple and Raisin Parcels
Serves 8

For the pastry

12 oz (350 g) plain flour, plus a little extra for rolling out

a pinch of salt

3 oz (75 g) softened pure lard, cut into smallish lumps

3 oz (75 g) softened butter, cut into smallish lumps

For the filling

8 oz (225 g) Bramley cooking apples (unpeeled), cored and cut into ½ inch (1 cm) dice

4 oz (110 g) Cox's apples (unpeeled), cored and cut into ½ inch (1 cm) dice

3 oz (75 g) raisins, soaked overnight in 4 fl oz (120 ml) dry cider

8 teaspoons semolina

16 whole cloves

2 oz (50 g) golden caster sugar, plus an extra teaspoon for sprinkling

1 large egg white, lightly beaten

You will also need a non-stick baking tin, 6 x 10 inches (15 x 25.5 cm), 1 inch (2.5 cm) deep.

This is yet another version of a good old apple pie, but the great thing about this recipe is that it bakes into individual portions, so it's much easier when you come to serve it. Raisins are a good winter addition, but in autumn you could replace them with 4 oz (110 g) of blackberries or, in summer, make the whole thing with 1 lb (450 g) of gooseberries, adding 3½ oz (95 g) sugar.

Start this recipe the night before by soaking the raisins in the cider. The next day, make the pastry, and to do this, sift the flour with the pinch of salt into a large bowl, holding the sieve high. Add the lard and butter and, using your fingertips, lightly rub the fats into the flour, lifting the mixture up to give it a good airing. When the mixture is crumbly, add about a tablespoon of cold water. Start mixing the pastry with a knife, then finish off with your hands, adding a little more water, till you have a smooth dough that leaves the bowl clean. Now pop it in a polythene bag and chill for 30 minutes.

Meanwhile, pre-heat the oven to gas mark 6, 400°F (200°C). Remove the pastry from the fridge, then divide it into 4 pieces. Dust your work surface lightly with flour, then roll each into a length about 5 x 10 inches (13 x 25.5 cm) and trim each piece into two 5 inch (13 cm) squares.

Working with 2 squares at a time, scatter a teaspoon of semolina over each pastry square, then mix both varieties of apple together and add 2 tablespoons of chopped apples, 2 cloves, 2 teaspoons of sugar and some drained raisins to each square. Now brush the edges of each square with some of the beaten egg white, then loosely fold the corners over. Then, using a fish slice to help you, lift each parcel into the tin, tucking them neatly into the corners, and repeat with the remaining squares so that they all fit snugly in the tin.

If you have any fruit left over, carefully lift the corners of each parcel and add some more apples and raisins. Now either leave the parcels open or squeeze the pastry corners together a little more. Next, brush the pastry with the remaining beaten egg white and scatter the rest of the sugar over, along with the extra teaspoon of sugar. Bake in the oven on the shelf just above the centre for 50 minutes, then serve warm with cream, ice cream or custard and don't forget to warn your guests that there are a few whole cloves lurking.

Note If you're using blackberries, gooseberries, rhubarb or blackcurrants, use a dessert-spoon of semolina in each parcel to absorb the extra juice.

Steamed Baked Puddings

Steamed Treacle Sponge Pudding
Serves 6-8

1 tablespoon black treacle

3 tablespoons golden syrup, plus
3-4 extra tablespoons, to serve

6 oz (175 g) self-raising flour

1 rounded teaspoon baking powder

6 oz (175 g) very soft butter

3 large eggs

6 oz (175 g) light brown soft sugar

You will also need a 2 pint
(1.2 litre) pudding basin, well
buttered, a double sheet of kitchen
foil, 12 x 16 inches (30 x 40 cm),
and some string.

In the winter, when the weather is getting you down or you're feeling grey or sad, I'm certain a steamed treacle sponge will put you right in no time at all. It takes moments to prepare, will steam away happily all by itself without needing attention, and is the ultimate in comfort foods.

First of all, measure the 3 tablespoons of golden syrup into the pudding basin (grease the spoon first). Now take a large mixing bowl, sift the flour and baking powder into it, add the soft butter, eggs, sugar and black treacle. Then use an electric hand whisk (or a large fork and a lot of elbow grease) and beat the mixture for about 2 minutes until it's thoroughly blended.

Now spoon the mixture into the basin and use the back of a spoon to level the top, then place the foil over the basin, making a pleat in the centre. Next, pull it down the outside of the basin and tie the string round the rim, taking it over the top and tying it on the other side to make yourself a handle for lifting. Then trim off the excess foil all the way round. Now place the pudding in a steamer fitted over a saucepan of boiling water and steam the pudding for 2 hours, checking the water level halfway through.

To serve, loosen the pudding all round, using a palette knife, invert it on to a warmed plate, and pour the extra 3-4 tablespoons of syrup (warmed, if you like) over the top before taking it to the table. Serve with custard or some well-chilled crème fraîche.

Queen of Puddings
Serves 4

1 pint (570 ml) milk

½ oz (10 g) butter

4 oz (110 g) fresh white
breadcrumbs

2 oz (50 g) golden caster sugar,
plus 1 teaspoon

grated zest of 1 small lemon

2 large eggs

3 tablespoons raspberry jam

You will also need a 1½ pint
(850 ml) oval pie dish, generously
buttered.

Pre-heat the oven to gas mark 4,
350°F (180°C).

This, with a cloud of meringue on top, is probably one of the lightest and most mouth-watering puddings ever invented.

First, pour the milk into a saucepan and bring to the boil. Remove from the heat and stir in the butter, breadcrumbs, 1 oz (25 g) of the sugar and the lemon zest, and leave for 20 minutes to allow the breadcrumbs to swell.

Now separate the eggs, lightly beat the yolks and add them to the cooled breadcrumb mixture. Pour it all into the pie dish and spread it out evenly. Bake in the centre of the oven for 30-35 minutes, or until set.

Meantime, in a small saucepan melt the raspberry jam over a low heat and, when the pudding is ready, remove it from the oven and spread the jam carefully and evenly all over the top.

Next, using an electric hand whisk, lightly beat the egg whites in a large scrupulously clean bowl until stiff, then whisk in 1 oz (25 g) of caster sugar and spoon this meringue mixture over the pudding. Finally, sprinkle the teaspoon of caster sugar over it all and bake for a further 10-15 minutes until the topping is golden brown.

Note If you want to serve eight people, double the ingredients, use a 3 pint (1.75 litre) baking dish and give both stages a fraction more cooking time.

Spotted Dick Rides Again
Serves 4-6

For the suet pastry

4 oz (110 g) self-raising flour, plus a little extra for rolling out

2 oz (50 g) fresh white broadorumbo

3 oz (75 g) shredded suet

a pinch of salt

2 fl oz (55 ml) milk

For the filling

6 oz (175 g) raisins

1 small Bramley cooking apple (about 6 oz/175 g), washed, cored and roughly chopped (no need to peel)

3 oz (75 g) dark brown soft sugar

grated zest of ½ lemon

You will also need a sheet of kitchen foil, 10 x 14 inches (25.5 x 35.5 cm).

This was once a very famous pudding, but it's now sadly forgotten. Just the thing to serve for Sunday lunch after a freezing cold, wintry walk. The perfect comfort pudding.

First of all, mix the filling ingredients together in a bowl. After that, make the suet pastry: sift the flour into a bowl, add the breadcrumbs, suet and pinch of salt, and mix to combine. Mix 2 fl oz (55 ml) water and the milk together and add a little to the dry ingredients, sprinkling it here and there. Now, using a flat-bladed knife, begin to mix, adding a little more liquid until the mixture looks as if it is coming together. Finish off, using your hands, adding drops of liquid until you end up with a smooth, elastic dough that feels moist.

Next, transfer the dough to a flat, lightly floured surface, roll it out to a rectangle roughly measuring 8 x 12 inches (20 x 30 cm) and dampen the edges with water. Then spread the filling evenly over it and roll it up gently and carefully from the narrow end. Now wrap the pudding in the kitchen foil, twisting it at each end to form a seal.

After that, fit a fan steamer (unscrew the central spindle) in a saucepan, add boiling water from a kettle and as soon as it comes back to the boil, pop the pudding in. Put a lid on and steam for 2 hours, keeping the water at a steady simmer, and making sure it is topped up if it needs it. Serve the pudding in warmed bowls, cut in thick slices, with custard – an absolutely essential accompaniment.

Steamed Raisin Pudding with Port Wine Sauce
Serves 4

8 oz (225 g) large raisins

2 oz (50 g) fresh white breadcrumbs

2 oz (50 g) self-raising flour, sifted

4 oz (110 g) shredded suet

⅛ teaspoon salt

½ whole nutmeg, freshly grated

½ teaspoon ground ginger

⅛ teaspoon ground mace

1 oz (25 g) mixed whole candied peel, finely chopped

grated zest of 1 orange

3 large eggs

3 tablespoons brandy

For the sauce

5 fl oz (150 ml) ruby or tawny port

grated zest of 1 Seville orange (but an ordinary orange will do)

2 oz (50 g) golden caster sugar

1 oz (25 g) soft unsalted butter

1 teaspoon plain flour

½ whole nutmeg, freshly grated

1 tablespoon Seville (or ordinary) orange juice

You will also need a 1½ pint (850 ml) pudding basin, well buttered, a double sheet of foil, 12 x 16 inches (30 x 40 cm), and some string.

This is a very special steamed pudding, but so easy to make. Don't worry about the absence of sugar – the raisins provide enough sweetness.

In a large bowl, mix together the breadcrumbs, flour and suet. Add the raisins, making sure there are none stuck together. When these ingredients are well mixed, add the salt, nutmeg, ginger, mace, candied peel and orange zest and again, mix thoroughly.

Now, in a small bowl, beat the eggs well and add them and the brandy to the mixture and stir for at least 5 minutes to amalgamate everything thoroughly and evenly. Pack the pudding basin with the mixture, and cover with the foil, making a pleat in the centre. Then pull it down the outside of the basin and tie down with string, taking it over the top and tying it on the other side to make yourself a handle for lifting. Trim off the excess foil all the way round. Now steam the pudding for 4 hours, making sure that the saucepan doesn't boil dry.

Meanwhile, to make the sauce, begin by simmering the orange zest, 5 fl oz (150 ml) of water and the sugar in a saucepan for 15 minutes until syrupy.

Now mix the butter into the flour and divide it up into about 6 pieces, adding them to the syrup at the end of the cooking time, followed by the port, nutmeg and orange juice. Simmer the mixture for 1 minute over a gentle heat, stirring continuously, then serve immediately. When ready to serve, loosen the pudding all round the sides with a palette knife and turn out on to a heated dish. Serve with the Port Wine Sauce.

Note The sauce can be prepared in advance, except for the butter and flour part, which should be added just before serving.

Bread and Butter Pudding
Serves 4-6

8 slices white bread (from a small loaf), buttered

½ oz (10 g) whole candied lemon or orange peel, finely chopped

2 oz (50 g) currants

10 fl oz (275 ml) milk

2½ fl oz (65 ml) double cream

2 oz (50 g) golden caster sugar

grated zest of ½ small lemon

3 large eggs

whole nutmeg for grating

You will also need a rectangular baking dish, 7 x 9 inches (18 x 23 cm), well buttered.

Pre-heat the oven to gas mark 4, 350°F (180°C).

This traditional English recipe is fragrant, soft, moist, wobbly beneath, and toasted and crunchy on top. I would go the whole hog and serve it with some chilled, untreated Jersey cream.

First of all, cut each slice of buttered bread in half and then into quarters, leaving the crusts on. Now arrange one layer of bread over the base of the dish, sprinkle over the candied peel and half the currants, then cover with another layer of bread and the remainder of the currants.

Next, in a measuring jug, measure out the milk and add the double cream. Stir in the sugar and lemon zest, then whisk the eggs, first on their own in a small bowl and then into the milk mixture.

Now pour the whole lot over the bread, grate some nutmeg over the surface, then bake on the centre shelf of the oven for 30-40 minutes, or until the top is golden brown and crusty. Remove it and leave for 5 minutes before serving.

Canary Lemon Sponge Puddings with Lemon Curd Cream
Serves 6

For the sponge puddings

grated zest of 1 lemon and
1 tablespoon lemon juice

4 oz (110 g) self-raising flour

1 teaspoon baking powder

4 oz (110 g) unsalted butter, at
room temperature, cut into
small pieces, plus a little extra
for greasing

2 large eggs

4 oz (110 g) golden caster sugar

For the lemon curd

grated zest and juice of 2 large
juicy lemons

2 large eggs

6 oz (175 g) golden caster sugar

4 oz (110 g) unsalted butter, at
room temperature, cut into small
pieces

1 teaspoon cornflour

For the lemon curd cream

half of the lemon curd

5 fl oz (150 ml) double cream

You will also need 6 mini pudding
basins, each with a capacity of
6 fl oz (175 ml), some kitchen foil
and baking parchment.

Canary Pudding is an old English steamed sponge pudding with jam. Because our football team is called the Canaries, I have adapted it to become a lemony version, so as to add a little canary colour. It's very popular in our restaurant at Norwich City Football Club. If you haven't got time to make the lemon curd, you can now buy some quite good ones – or use jam and serve with custard.

Begin by making the lemon curd. To do this, start by lightly whisking the eggs in a medium saucepan, then add the rest of the ingredients and place the saucepan over a medium heat. Now whisk continuously, using a balloon whisk, until the mixture thickens – about 7-8 minutes. Next, lower the heat to its minimum setting and let the curd gently simmer for a further minute, continuing to whisk. After that, remove it from the heat.

Next, butter the basins well and place a round piece of well-buttered baking parchment in the bottom of each one. Then take a large mixing bowl and sift the flour and baking powder into it, holding the sieve high to give the flour a good airing. Next, add the butter, eggs, sugar, lemon zest and juice. Then, using an electric hand whisk, beat the mixture for about a minute until it is thoroughly blended.

After that, divide the lemon curd in half and share one half among the basins, filling each one with about a dessertspoon of lemon curd. Then spoon in the sponge mixture, dividing it equally among the basins and levelling the tops. Then place a piece of kitchen foil over each one, making a pleat in the centre and twisting the edges all round.

Now place a saucepan over the heat and add boiling water from the kettle. When it comes back to the boil, arrange the puddings in a steamer (you'll have to stack them on top of each other) and fit it over the saucepan. Pop a lid on and steam them for about 25 minutes, keeping the water at a steady simmer. They are ready when the centres spring back when pressed lightly.

While the puddings are cooking, you can make the lemon curd cream. All you do is place the other half of the lemon curd in a saucepan, add 5 fl oz

(150 ml) water and the cream, and then heat very gently, stirring all the time, until hot but not bubbling. Then pour it into a warmed serving jug and keep warm.

When the puddings are cooked, remove the kitchen foil and loosen them all round with a small palette knife. Then turn them out on to warmed serving plates, remove the paper discs and pour a little sauce over each one or hand it round separately.

Apple and Orange Crunch
Serves 4

3 small Bramley cooking apples (each about 8 oz/225 g), peeled and sliced thinly

½ the zest and all the juice of 1 small orange

4 oz (110 g) butter

approximately 10 thinnish slices of bread from a white day-old loaf or a small brown wholemeal loaf

3 oz (75 g) demerara sugar

You will also need a baking dish 6 x 8 inches (15 x 20 cm), 2 inches (5 cm) deep, well buttered.

Pre-heat the oven to gas mark 4, 350°F (180°C).

I like this crunchy pudding served with proper custard sauce or, failing that, a thick, chilled pouring cream.

Melt the butter in a saucepan over a low heat. Cut the crusts off the bread slices and, using a pastry brush, spread 6 or 7 on both sides with melted butter (reserving some for the rest). Place them in the baking dish, covering the base and sides as a lining. Press them down firmly, then sprinkle in a layer of sliced apple, a little of the orange zest and juice, and a layer of sugar. Carry on like this until all the apple is used, but keep back a tablespoon of sugar.

Brush melted butter on the other slices of bread and press them on top. Sprinkle on the remaining sugar and add any melted butter that's left over.

Bake the pudding for 50-55 minutes or until the top is crisp, golden and crunchy, and the apples inside are soft.

Sticky Gingerbread Puddings
with Ginger Wine and Brandy Sauce
Serves 8

4 oz (110 g) stem ginger in syrup (8 pieces)

1 heaped teaspoon freshly grated ginger

6 oz (175 g) self raising flour

¼ teaspoon ground ginger

⅓ teaspoon ground cinnamon

⅓ teaspoon ground cloves

½ teaspoon baking powder

¾ teaspoon bicarbonate of soda

2 large eggs

3 oz (75 g) soft butter

4 oz (110 g) molasses sugar

1 tablespoon black treacle

6 oz (175 g) Bramley cooking apple, peeled, cored and chopped small

For the sauce

4 tablespoons ginger wine

2 tablespoons brandy

6 oz (175 g) dark brown soft sugar

4 oz (110 g) unsalted butter

2 pieces of stem ginger, chopped small

You will also need 8 mini pudding basins, each with a capacity of 6 fl oz (175 ml), well buttered, and a solid baking sheet.

Pre-heat the oven to gas mark 4, 350°F (180°C).

This has the same degree of lightness as the Sticky Toffee Puddings (page 65) and the fragrance and spiciness of preserved ginger takes the edge off the sweetness beautifully.

First of all, place the 8 pieces of stem ginger in a food processor and turn the motor on for about 7-10 seconds. Be careful not to process for too long – the ginger should be chopped small, but not puréed! After that, sift the flour, ground spices, baking powder and bicarbonate of soda into a mixing bowl. Then add the eggs, butter and sugar. The way to deal with the treacle is to grease the spoon first and, using a spatula or another spoon, push it into the bowl to join the rest of the ingredients. Now add the freshly grated ginger, then, using an electric hand whisk, whisk everything together gradually, adding 6 fl oz (175 ml) warm water until you have a smooth mixture. Finally, fold in the apple and stem ginger. Now divide the mixture among the buttered pudding basins, stand them on the baking sheet and bake in the centre of the oven for 35 minutes, or until they feel firm and springy to the touch. Then remove them from the oven and let them stand for about 5 minutes, run a small palette knife around the edges of the basins and turn them out on to a heatproof dish or tray.

To make the sauce, all you do is gently melt together the sugar and butter until all the granules of sugar have completely dissolved, then whisk in the ginger wine and brandy, add the chopped ginger and the sauce is then ready. To serve the puddings, pre-heat the grill to its highest setting. Spoon the sauce over them, making sure that no little bits of ginger are actually on the top of the puddings, then place the whole thing under the grill, so that the tops of the puddings are about 5 inches (13 cm) from the source of heat. Now allow them to heat through, which will take about 5 minutes, by which time the tops will be slightly crunchy and the sauce will be hot and bubbly. Serve with chilled pouring cream.

Note If you want to make these puddings in advance, turn them out on to a heatproof dish or tray and leave them to get completely cold, keep them wrapped in clingfilm until you need them. Then grill, as described above – they will take about 8 minutes to heat through. These also freeze beautifully and, after defrosting, should be reheated in the same way.

Sticky Gingerbread Puddings with
Ginger Wine and Brandy Sauce

Old English Apple Hat
Serves 6-8

For the suet pastry

8 oz (225 g) self-raising flour, plus a little extra for rolling out

4 oz (110 g) shredded suet

a pinch of salt

For the filling

1 lb (450 g) Bramley cooking apples (weight after coring), washed (no need to peel)

8 oz (225 g) Cox's apples (weight after coring), washed (no need to peel)

2 oz (50 g) golden caster sugar

6 cloves

You will also need a 2½ pint (1.5 litre) pudding basin, very well buttered, a double sheet of kitchen foil, 10 inches (25.5 cm) square, and some string.

If it's true there's 'a time for everything under Heaven', then midwinter is quite definitely the most appropriate time to make an old-fashioned steamed pudding. There's nothing wrong with a cold, grey month in the calendar when it can justify such wonderful culinary indulgence. Here, I am offering you the real thing – a soft, steamy suet crust encasing fragrant and luscious apples, with a hint of cloves. It's no trouble at all to make, and you can leave it gently steaming away, knowing all that soothing, comforting pleasure is awaiting you.

To make the suet pastry, all you do is sift the flour into a bowl, add the suet and pinch of salt and mix them together. Now start to add a little cold water, sprinkling it here and there. Then take a flat-bladed knife and begin to mix with it, still adding water, until the mixture looks like it is coming together. Finish off using your hands, adding drops of water until you get a smooth, elastic dough. There's no need to rest the dough, so you can straightaway reserve a quarter of the pastry (for the lid) and then roll the rest out on a flat, lightly floured surface to a 10 inch (25.5 cm) round, giving it quarter-turns as you roll to keep the round shape. Now transfer the pastry to the pudding basin and arrange it to form a lining, using your hands to press it round as evenly as possible. If you have some pastry above the rim, just squeeze it down to form a neat edge.

Next, cut the apples into quarters. Now slice them into ½ inch (1 cm) chunks and, as you add them to the basin, sprinkle in the sugar and tuck in a clove here and there. Pack the apples down as you go and don't worry if they rise a bit above the top, as they will shrink in the cooking.

Now roll out the reserved pastry to form the lid, dampen the edge all round with water, then place it over the apples. Press the edge all round to weld it to the edge of the pastry lining the basin. After that, take the double sheet of kitchen foil, make a pleat in the centre and cover the top of the pudding with it. Then tie it securely with string around the top of the basin, and make a string handle (to help you lift it into the steamer) by attaching a length of string to both sides. Now boil a kettle and pour the boiling water into a saucepan to about halfway, place it over a medium heat and, when it comes back to the boil, fit a steamer over the top. Pop the pudding in, put the lid on and steam the pudding for exactly 2 hours, keeping the water at a steady simmer. After an hour, check the water level in the saucepan and, if necessary, top up with boiling water.

To serve the pudding, remove the string and kitchen foil, loosen the pudding all round with a palette knife, then turn it out on to a warmed plate. Serve cut into slices, with the apples strewn around the pastry and – it has to be said – lots of proper custard.

Old-fashioned Rice Pudding
Serves 4-6

4 fl oz (120 ml) pudding rice

1 x 410 g tin evaporated milk

1 pint (570 ml) whole milk

1½ oz (40 g) golden granulated or caster sugar

1 whole nutmeg

1 oz (25 g) butter

You will also need a round ovenproof dish with a diameter of 9 inches (23 cm), 2 inches (5 cm) deep, lightly buttered.

Pre-heat the oven to gas mark 2, 300°F (150°C).

This is the real thing – a mass of creamy rice and a thick brown speckled nutmeg skin. Don't forget to take a sharp knife and scrape off all the bits of caramelised skin that stick to the edges – my grandmother always did that and gave everyone an equal amount.

This recipe is simplicity itself, because all you do is mix the evaporated milk and whole milk together in a jug, then place the rice and sugar in the ovenproof dish, pour in the liquid and give it all a good stir. Grate the whole nutmeg all over the surface (it may seem a lot but it needs it), then, finally, dot the butter on top in little flecks.

Next, just carefully pop the dish in the oven on the centre shelf and leave it there for 30 minutes, then slide the shelf out and give everything a good stir. Repeat the stirring after a further 30 minutes, then pop the dish back in the oven to cook for another hour, this time without stirring. At the end of this time the rice grains will have become swollen, with pools of creamy liquid all around them, and, of course, all that lovely skin! This is wonderful served warm.

St Stephen's Pudding
Serves 4

4 oz (110 g) white breadcrumbs

2 oz (50 g) self-raising flour, sifted

2 oz (50 g) light brown soft sugar

3 oz (75 g) shredded suet

a pinch of salt

4 oz (110 g) seedless raisins

2 medium Bramley cooking apples, peeled and grated

grated zest of 1 lemon

1 large egg

3 tablespoons milk

You will also need a 2 pint (1.2 litre) pudding basin, well buttered, some baking parchment, kitchen foil, and some string.

This was sent to me by a television viewer in East Anglia and is a very good alternative if you prefer a less rich pudding for Christmas.

In a large mixing bowl, first combine all the dry ingredients, including the pinch of salt, then add the raisins, the grated apples and the grated lemon zest. Stir thoroughly to combine everything well. Now beat the egg into the milk and stir the whole lot into the mixture.

Pack the mixture into the pudding basin, cover the basin tightly with a sheet of baking parchment, then with a sheet of foil make a pleat in the centre and secure with string. After that, boil a kettle and pour the boiling water into a saucepan, about half full, place it on a medium heat and, when it comes back to the boil, fit a steamer over the top. Steam the pudding for 2 hours, checking the water level in the saucepan now and then. Serve with custard, or at Christmas with rum butter.

Spiced Bread Pudding with Brandy Cream
Serves 6

For the bread pudding

2 teaspoons ground mixed spice

8 oz (225 g) white or brown bread, crusts removed

4 oz (110 g) sultanas

1 oz (25 g) currants

1 oz (25 g) raisins

2 oz (50 g) whole candied lemon or orange peel, chopped

3 tablespoons brandy

10 fl oz (275 ml) milk

2 oz (50 g) butter

3 oz (75 g) dark brown soft sugar

1 large egg, beaten

grated zest of ½ orange

grated zest of 1 lemon

1 tablespoon demerara sugar

whole nutmeg for grating

For the brandy cream

1 dessertspoon brandy

5 fl oz (150 ml) double cream

1 oz (25 g) golden caster sugar

You will also need a baking dish, 6¼ x 8 inches (15.5 x 20 cm), 1¾ inches (4.5 cm) deep, buttered.

Sometimes this gets confused with bread-and-butter pudding, but it's quite different. It was invented, I think, to use up stale bread, which is still a good reason for making it – however, it has developed into something so wonderful, it's worth letting the bread go stale on purpose.

Begin by placing the sultanas, currants, raisins and candied peel in a bowl. Pour over the brandy and leave aside to marinate. Then, in a large bowl, break the bread into ½ inch (1 cm) pieces. Add the milk, then give the mixture a good stir and leave it for about 30 minutes so the bread becomes well soaked. Pre-heat the oven to gas mark 4, 350°F (180°C).

Next, melt the butter and mix it with the dark brown soft sugar, mixed spice and beaten egg and then add to the second bowl. Now, using a fork, beat the mixture well, making sure there are no large lumps, then stir in the marinated fruits, with any brandy remaining, and also the orange and lemon zests.

After that, spread the mixture in the baking dish and sprinkle the sugar over it, along with some freshly grated nutmeg. Bake on the centre shelf of the oven for about 1¼ hours. Meanwhile, whisk together the ingredients for the brandy cream and serve it with the pudding warm from the oven.

Chunky Marmalade Bread and Butter Pudding
Serves 4-6

2 rounded tablespoons dark chunky orange marmalade

6 slices white bread, from a good-quality large loaf, ½ inch (1 cm) thick with crusts left on

2 oz (50 g) softened butter

10 fl oz (275 ml) whole milk

2½ fl oz (65 ml) double cream

3 large eggs

3 oz (75 g) golden caster sugar

grated zest of 1 large orange

1 tablespoon demerara sugar

1 oz (25 g) mixed whole candied peel, finely chopped

You will also need a baking dish, 7 x 9 inches (18 x 23 cm), 2 inches (5 cm) deep, lightly buttered.

Pre-heat the oven to gas mark 4, 350°F (180°C).

Is there anyone, anywhere who doesn't like bread and butter pudding? If you're a devoted fan, then this is bread and butter pudding as you've always known it, but with the added extra of Seville orange marmalade, chunky candied peel and grated orange zest – a delightfully different combination, which produces another winning version of an old-time favourite.

First, generously butter the slices of bread on one side, then spread the marmalade on 3 of these slices, and put the other 3 slices on top (buttered side down) so you've got 3 rounds of sandwiches. Now spread some butter over the top slice of each sandwich and cut each one into quarters to make little triangles or squares.

Then arrange the sandwiches, butter side up, overlapping each other in the baking dish and standing almost upright. After that, whisk the milk, cream, eggs and sugar together and pour this all over the bread. Scatter the surface of the bread with the grated orange zest, demerara sugar and candied peel, then place the pudding on a high shelf and bake it for 35-40 minutes until it's puffy and golden and the top crust is crunchy.

Serve the pudding straight from the oven while it's still puffy, with either crème fraîche or chilled pouring cream.

Little Sticky Toffee Puddings with Pecan Toffee Sauce
Serves 8

6 oz (175 g) pitted dates, chopped

½ teaspoon pure vanilla extract

2 teaspoons coffee essence

¾ teaspoon bicarbonate of soda

3 oz (75 g) soft butter

5 oz (150 g) golden caster sugar

2 large eggs, beaten

6 oz (175 g) self-raising flour, sifted

For the sauce

1 oz (25 g) pecan nuts, chopped

6 oz (175 g) soft brown sugar

4 oz (110 g) butter

6 tablespoons double cream

You will also need 8 mini pudding basins, each with a capacity of 6 fl oz (175 ml), or eight 3 inch (7.5 cm) ramekins, lightly oiled with a flavourless oil, a Swiss-roll tin, and a baking sheet.

Pre-heat the oven to gas mark 4, 350°F (180°C).

This is as wicked as it sounds. A truly delectable combination of flavours and textures that are light and melt in the mouth. I would choose this as a dinner party dessert, as the puddings freeze well like the Sticky Gingerbread Puddings (see page 50) and are no trouble to reheat. After freezing, defrost, pour the hot sauce over and grill them.

Begin by putting the chopped dates in a bowl and pouring 6 fl oz (175 ml) boiling water over them. Then add the vanilla extract, coffee essence and bicarbonate of soda and leave on one side. Next, in a large mixing bowl, cream the butter and sugar together, beating (preferably with an electric hand whisk) until the mixture is pale, light and fluffy. Now gradually add the beaten eggs, a little at a time, beating well after each addition. After that, carefully and lightly fold in the sifted flour, using a metal spoon, and then you can fold in the date mixture (including the liquid). You'll probably think at this stage that you've done something wrong, because the mixture will look very sloppy, but don't worry: that is perfectly correct and the slackness of the mixture is what makes the puddings so light. Now divide the mixture equally among the 8 containers, place them on the baking sheet and bake in the centre of the oven for 25 minutes.

When they're cooked, leave them to cool for 5 minutes, then, using a cloth to protect your hands, slide a small palette knife around each pudding and turn them out. If they have risen too much you may have to slice a little off the bottoms so that they can sit evenly on the plate. Now place the puddings on the shallow Swiss-roll tin.

Next, make the sauce by combining all the ingredients in a saucepan and heating very gently until the sugar has melted and all the crystals have dissolved.

To serve: pre-heat the grill to its highest setting, and pour the sauce evenly over the puddings. Place the tin under the grill, so the tops of the puddings are about 5 inches (13 cm) from the heat (knock off any nuts on the top to prevent them browning) and let the puddings heat through for 8 minutes. What will happen is the tops will become brown and slightly crunchy and the sauce will be hot and bubbling. Serve with chilled pouring cream – and sit back to watch the looks of ecstasy on the faces of your guests.

Steamed Panettone Pudding with Eliza Acton's Hot Punch Sauce
Serves 6

For the steamed panettone pudding

3 x 100 g panettone cakes or the same amount from a 500 g panettone cake

6 oz (175 g) dried mixed fruit, soaked in 3 tablespoons rum overnight

2 oz (50 g) whole almonds (with skins left on)

2 oz (50 g) mixed whole candied peel, finely chopped

grated zest of 1 orange

grated zest of 2 lemons

2 oz (50 g) molasses sugar

10 fl oz (275 ml) milk

5 fl oz (150 ml) double cream

3 large eggs

For Eliza Acton's hot punch sauce

1 large orange

1 lemon

4 oz (110 g) golden caster sugar

1 oz (25 g) plain flour

2 oz (50 g) soft unsalted butter

2 tablespoons rum

2 tablespoons brandy

6 fl oz (175 ml) medium sherry

You will also need a 2 pint (1.2 litre) pudding basin, well buttered, and a double sheet of kitchen foil, 10 inches (25.5 cm) square, and some string.

Panettone is an Italian fruit bread that's sold in England mostly in the autumn and around Christmas time in beautifully designed boxes with carrying ribbons. If you would like a light but quite delectable alternative to Christmas pudding, this is it. I've tried making it in advance, freezing and then re-heating it, and it works beautifully. But don't confine it to Christmas, as it's a truly great steamed pudding to serve at any time, particularly with Victorian writer Eliza Acton's extremely alcoholic citrus sauce.

You need to begin this by soaking the dried mixed fruit in the rum overnight. The next day, toast the almonds. To do this, pre-heat the grill to its highest setting for 10 minutes, then place the almonds on some foil and toast them under the grill for 2-3 minutes, but don't go away, as they will burn very quickly. When they look nicely toasted and browned on one side, turn them all over and toast the other side, then remove them from the grill and leave them aside to cool.

Next, cut the panettone into 1 inch (2.5 cm) chunks and place them in a large mixing bowl, along with the candied peel, orange and lemon zests and the soaked, dried mixed fruit and any drops of rum that didn't get soaked up. Now chop the almonds into thin slivers and add these. Then give it all a really good stir to distribute everything evenly.

Next, in another bowl, whisk together the sugar, milk, cream and eggs and pour this all over the panettone, giving everything another good mix. Now pour the mixture into the buttered pudding basin and press everything down to pack it in. Then cover the top of the pudding with the double sheet of foil and tie it securely with the string round the top of the basin, then make a string handle by taking a length of string over the top of the pudding basin and attaching it to each side – this will help you lift the pudding into the steamer. Now boil a kettle and pour the boiling water into the saucepan, about half full, place it on a medium heat and, when it comes back to the boil, fit a steamer over the top.

Now pop the pudding in, put the lid on and steam the pudding for exactly

2 hours. After 1 hour, check the water level in the saucepan and, if necessary, top it up with boiling water. If you are using a fan steamer, put in enough water to just reach the steamer, and you'll need to top it up 2 or 3 times.

Meanwhile, make the hot punch sauce. First, you need to prepare orange and lemon zests, and to do this it's best to use a potato peeler and pare off the outer zest, leaving the white pith behind. What you need is 4 strips of each zest measuring approximately 1 x 2 inches (2.5 x 5 cm). Then, using a sharp knife, cut the strips into very thin, needle-like shreds. Now pop these into a medium saucepan, along with the sugar and 10 fl oz (275 ml) water, bring everything up to a slow simmer and let it simmer as gently as possible for 15 minutes. While that is happening, squeeze the juice from the orange and lemon, and in a separate bowl, mix the flour and butter together to form a paste. When the 15 minutes are up, add the orange and lemon juice, along with the rum, brandy and sherry, and bring it all back up to a gentle simmer. Now add the paste to the liquid in small, peanut-sized pieces, whisking as you add them, until they have dissolved and the sauce has thickened. Serve the sauce hot in a warmed serving jug, and, if you make it in advance, reheat it gently without letting it come to the boil.

To serve the pudding, remove the foil and string and let it stand for 5-10 minutes, then slide a palette knife all round to loosen it and turn it out on to a warmed plate. Pour some of the hot punch sauce over the pudding and carry it to the table, with the rest of the sauce in a jug to hand round separately.

Baked Apple and Almond Pudding
Serves 4-6

1 lb (450 g) Bramley cooking apples, peeled, cored and sliced

4 oz (110 g) ground almonds

2 oz (50 g) soft brown sugar

4 oz (110 g) butter, at room temperature

4 oz (110 g) golden caster sugar

2 large eggs, beaten

You will also need a round, ovenproof baking dish with a diameter of 8 inches (20 cm), 1¾ inches (4.5 cm) deep, buttered.

Pre-heat the oven to gas mark 4, 350°F (180°C).

Since this recipe was given to me many years ago by the proprietor of the Sign of the Angel in Laycock, it has become really popular with readers, as I know from their many letters.

Place the apples in a saucepan with the brown sugar and approximately 2 tablespoons of water, simmer gently until soft, and then arrange them in the bottom of the prepared baking dish.

In a mixing bowl, cream the butter and caster sugar until pale and fluffy and then beat in the eggs a little at a time. When all the egg is in, carefully and lightly fold in the ground almonds. Now spread this mixture over the apples, and even out the surface with the back of a tablespoon. Then bake on a highish shelf in the oven for exactly 1 hour.

This pudding is equally good served warm or cold – either way, it's nice with some chilled pouring cream. Once cooled, it will keep in the fridge for 3 or 4 days.

Tarts

Cheesecakes

Pancakes

Deep Lemon Tart
Serves 6-8

For the pastry

6 oz (175 g) plain flour

1½ oz (40 g) icing sugar

3 oz (75 g) softened butter

a pinch of salt

1 large egg, separated

For the filling

6-8 lemons

6 large eggs

6 oz (175 g) golden caster sugar

7 fl oz (200 ml) whipping cream

To serve

a little icing sugar

crème fraîche

You will also need a deep, loose-based fluted tart tin, 9 inches (23 cm) in diameter, and 1½ inches (4 cm) deep, lightly oiled, and a solid baking sheet.

I once spent a great deal of time trying every sort of lemon tart imaginable in order to come up with the definitive version. And here it is – thicker than is usual which, quite rightly I think, includes much more filling than pastry. If you want to serve it warm you can prepare everything in advance – and pour the filling in just before you bake it.

The best way to make the pastry is in a food processor. To do this, add all the pastry ingredients (except the egg white) to the bowl with 1 tablespoon water and process until it forms a firm dough. Then turn it out and knead lightly before placing in a polythene bag and leaving in the fridge for 30 minutes to rest. To cook the pastry base, pre-heat the oven to gas mark 6, 400°F (200°C) and place the solid baking sheet inside to pre-heat as well. Now roll out the pastry as thinly as possible and carefully line the tart tin, pressing the pastry around the base and sides so that it comes about ¼ inch (5 mm) above the edge of the tin. Then prick the base with a fork and brush it all over with the reserved egg white, which you should lightly beat first. Bake on the baking sheet on the middle shelf for 20 minutes, then, as you remove it, turn the temperature down to gas mark 4, 350°F (180°C).

To make the filling, grate the zest from 6 of the lemons, and squeeze enough juice (you may need 8 lemons) to give 10 fl oz (275 ml). Now break the eggs into a bowl, add the sugar and whisk to combine, but don't overdo it or the eggs will thicken. Next, add the lemon juice and zest, followed by the cream, and whisk lightly. Now pour it all into a 2 pint (1.2 litre) jug.

The easiest way to fill the tart is to place the pastry case on the baking sheet in the oven, and then pour the filling straight into the pastry (this avoids having to carry the tart to the oven and spilling it). Bake for about 30 minutes or until the tart is set and feels springy in the centre. Let it cool for about half an hour if you want to serve it warm. It's also extremely good served chilled. Either way, dust it with icing sugar just before serving and serve with well-chilled crème fraîche.

Banoffee Cheesecake with Toffee Pecan Sauce

Serves 6-8

For the base

3 oz (75 g) pecan nuts (use half for the base and half for the sauce)

4 oz (110 g) sweet oat biscuits

1½ oz (40 g) melted butter

For the filling

3 medium, ripe bananas
(8 oz/225 g peeled weight)

1 tablespoon lemon juice

3 large eggs

12 oz (350 g) medium-fat curd cheese

1 x 200 g tub fromage frais
(8 per cent fat)

6 oz (175 g) golden caster sugar

For the sauce

2 oz (50 g) butter

3 oz (75 g) soft brown sugar

2 oz (50 g) granulated sugar

5 oz (150 g) golden syrup

5 fl oz (150 ml) double cream

a few drops of pure vanilla extract

For the topping

2 tablespoons lemon juice

3 medium, ripe bananas

You will also need a springform cake tin, 8 inches (20 cm) in diameter, lightly buttered.

Pre-heat the oven to gas mark 6, 400°F (200ºC).

The magic word 'banoffee' does not, as you might have thought, have exotic origins: it is simply an amalgam of banana and toffee. But it is magic nonetheless – the combination of bananas, cream and toffee is inspired. Here, I have incorporated them all into a cheesecake with the addition of one extra star ingredient, toasted pecan nuts.

Begin by toasting all the pecan nuts. Place them on a baking tray and bake in the oven for 6-8 minutes until lightly toasted or, if you watch them like a hawk, you can toast them under a grill. Then chop them quite small. Put the biscuits in a polythene bag, lay them flat and then roll them with a rolling pin to crush them coarsely. Then tip them into a bowl and add the melted butter and half the nuts. Mix them well, then press all this into the bottom of the cake tin and pre-bake the base in the oven for 10 minutes. Then lower the temperature to gas mark 2, 300°F (150°C).

For the filling, first blend the 3 bananas and lemon juice in a food processor until smooth, then simply add all the rest of the filling ingredients. Blend again, then pour it all over the biscuit base and bake on the middle shelf of the oven for 1 hour. Turn off the oven and leave the cheesecake inside to cool slowly until completely cold; this slow cooling will stop the cheesecake cracking.

To make the sauce, place the butter, sugars and syrup in a saucepan and, over a very low heat, allow everything to dissolve completely. Let it cook for about 5 minutes. Pour in the cream and vanilla extract and stir until everything is smooth, then add the rest of the chopped pecan nuts. Remove it from the heat and allow it to cool completely before pouring it into a jug ready for serving.

When you are ready to assemble the cheesecake, put the 2 tablespoons of lemon juice into a bowl. Slice the remaining bananas at an oblique angle into ¼ inch (5 mm) slices, and gently toss them around to get an even coating of juice. If you like, you can spoon a small circle of sauce into the centre, then layer the bananas in overlapping circles all round it. Serve the cheesecake, cut into slices, with the rest of the sauce handed round separately.

Classic Crepes Suzette
Serves 6

For the crepes

4 oz (110 g) plain flour

a pinch of salt

2 large eggs

7 fl oz (200 ml) milk, mixed
with 3 fl oz (75 ml) water

grated zest of 1 medium orange

1 tablespoon golden caster sugar

2 oz (50 g) butter, melted

For the sauce

5 fl oz (150 ml) orange juice (from
3-4 medium oranges)

grated zest of 1 medium orange

grated zest and juice of 1 small
lemon

1 tablespoon golden caster sugar

3 tablespoons Grand Marnier,
Cointreau or brandy, plus a little
extra, if you are going to flame
the pancakes

2 oz (50 g) unsalted butter

You will also need 2 solid-based
frying pans, one with a 7 inch
(18 cm) base diameter and the
other with a 10 inch (25.5 cm)
base, some kitchen paper and
greaseproof paper.

This is a qualifier for my 1960s recipe revival. There was a time when this recipe was certainly overexposed, but now that it has become a forgotten rarity, we can all re-appreciate its undoubted charm, which remains in spite of changes in fashion.

First of all, to make the crepes, sift the flour and salt into a large mixing bowl with the sieve held high above the bowl so the flour gets an airing.

Now make a well in the centre of the flour and break the eggs into it. Then begin whisking the eggs – any sort of whisk or even a fork will do – incorporating any bits of flour from around the edge of the bowl as you do so. Next, gradually add small quantities of the milk and water mixture, still whisking (don't worry about any lumps – they will eventually disappear as you whisk). When all the liquid has been added, use a rubber spatula to scrape any elusive bits of flour from around the edge into the centre. Then, add the orange zest and caster sugar and whisk once more until the batter is smooth, with the consistency of thin cream. Now spoon 2 tablespoons of the melted butter into the batter and whisk it in, then pour the rest into a bowl and use it as needed to lubricate the 7 inch (18 cm) pan, using a wodge of kitchen paper to smear it round.

Next, get the 7 inch (18 cm) pan really hot, then turn the heat down to medium and, to start with, do a test crepe to see if you're using the correct amount of batter. I find 1½ tablespoons about right. It's also helpful if you spoon the batter into a ladle so it can be poured into the hot pan in one go. As soon as the batter hits the hot pan, tip it around from side to side to get the base evenly coated with batter. It should take only half a minute or so to cook; you can lift the edge with a palette knife to see if it's tinged gold as it should be. Flip the crepe over with a fish slice or palette knife – the other side will need a few seconds only – then simply slide it out of the pan on to a plate. If they look a bit ragged in the pan, no matter, because they are going to be folded anyway. You should end up with 15-16 crepes, and, as you make them, stack them between sheets of greaseproof paper.

For the sauce, mix all the ingredients – with the exception of the butter – in a bowl. At the same time, warm the plates on which the crepes are going to be served.

Now melt the butter in the larger frying pan, pour in the sauce and allow it to heat very gently. Then place the first crepe in the pan and give it time to warm through before folding it in half and then half again to make a triangular shape. Slide this on to the very edge of the pan, tilt the pan slightly so the sauce runs back into the centre, then add the next crepe. Continue like this until they're all re-heated, folded and well soaked with the sauce.

You can flame them at this point if you like. Heat a ladle by holding it over a gas flame or by resting it on the edge of a hotplate, then, away from the heat, pour a little liqueur or brandy into it, return it to the heat to warm the spirit, then set light to it. Carry the flaming ladle to the table over the pan and pour the flames over the crepes before serving on the warmed plates.

Classic Crepes Suzette

Lucy's Tarte Tatin
Serves 6

For the pastry

4 oz (110 g) plain flour, plus a little extra for rolling out

1 oz (25 g) unsalted butter, at room temperature, cut into smallish lumps

1 oz (25 g) pure lard, at room temperature, cut into smallish lumps

For the filling

8 large Golden Delicious apples

3 oz (75 g) softened unsalted butter

6 oz (175 g) golden caster sugar

You will also need a non-stick, heavy-based frying pan that is ovenproof (including the handle), with a base diameter of 9½ inches (24 cm), 1½ inches (4 cm) deep.

Lucy Crabb, former Executive Chef at our restaurant at Norwich City Football Club, makes the very best *tarte Tatin* (caramelised apple flan) I've ever tasted. She insists on French apples for this great classic from the Loire Valley, but if you want to use English apples, such as Cox's, it will still be wonderful.

First of all, you need to make the pastry, so it has time to rest. Begin by sifting the flour into a large mixing bowl from a height, then cut the fats into the flour with a knife, before rubbing the mixture lightly with your fingertips, lifting everything up and letting it fall back into the bowl to give it a good airing. When the mixture reaches the crumb stage, sprinkle in enough water, 2-3 tablespoons, to bring it together to a smooth dough that leaves the sides of the bowl absolutely clean, with no crumbs left. Give it a light knead to bring it fully together, then place the pastry in a polythene bag and chill it in the fridge for 30 minutes.

To make the filling, peel the apples and then cut them in half vertically and remove the core. (Lucy does this with a melon baller, which works brilliantly and keeps the centre very neat.) Next, spread the softened butter evenly over the base of the pan and sprinkle the sugar over the top. Then, place the apples in concentric circles, cut side up. When you get to the centre, you may have to cut them into quarters to fill any gaps. Now you need to place the pan over a low heat so the butter and sugar melt very slowly together, which will take 8-10 minutes in all. When they have melted, increase the heat slightly, as you now want the sugar to caramelise. Gently shake the pan from time to time, so the apples don't stick and burn on the bottom. (Lucy insists this is not a dessert you can walk away from, as the minute you do, the sugar will burn.) Meanwhile, preheat the oven to gas mark 7, 425°F (220°C). It will take about 20-25 minutes for the sugar to reach a rich amber colour and, by that time, the apples should be soft but still retain their shape. When that has happened, remove the pan from the heat.

Now remove the pastry from the fridge, transfer it to a flat, lightly floured surface and roll it out to an 11½ inch (29 cm) round. Fit it over the top of the pan, allowing some to tuck down at the edge, which doesn't have to be too neat. Prick the pastry base all over with a fork so the steam is released when it's cooking and the pastry doesn't go soggy. Next, place the pan on the centre shelf of the oven and bake the tart for 20-25 minutes, or until the pastry is crisp and golden brown.

Remove it from the oven, using really thick oven gloves, and allow it to cool for about 5 minutes. Now the whole thing gets interesting. Take a plate or tray larger than the pan and place it over the top. Then, using an oven glove to hold the handle, invert the pan on to the plate, giving it a little shake before you do. Serve the tart warm, with lashings of crème fraîche. I have to say, any left over is still wonderful served cold.

Linzertorte
Serves 6-8

For the pastry

6 oz (175 g) plain flour, plus extra for rolling out

3 oz (75 g) blanched hazelnuts, ground in a food processor

2 oz (50 g) icing sugar, sifted

finely grated zest of 1 lemon

¼ teaspoon ground cinnamon

whole nutmeg for grating

4 oz (110 g) cold butter, cut into small pieces

2 large egg yolks, lightly beaten together with a fork

For the filling

12 oz (350 g) jellied cranberry sauce, or cranberry jelly is also brilliant

2 teaspoons lemon juice

a little icing sugar, to dust

You will also need a loose-based, fluted tart tin with a diameter of 9 inches (23 cm), buttered, and a medium, solid baking tray.

This is a famous Austrian torte named after the town of Linz. The rich pastry flan is made with ground hazelnuts. The fruity element is usually either redcurrant or raspberry, but a while ago I tried using cranberry jelly instead and liked the result very much.

First, combine the flour, ground hazelnuts, icing sugar, lemon zest, cinnamon and a few gratings of whole nutmeg in a mixing bowl, then rub in the butter until the mixture is crumbly. Stir in the egg yolks and form the mixture into a dough, then place it in a polythene bag and leave it in the fridge for 20 minutes to rest.

Pre-heat the oven to gas mark 5, 375°F (190°C) and pop the baking tray in to heat at the same time. Next, weigh a 5 oz (150 g) piece of the pastry dough and put it on one side. Then roll out the rest of the pastry on a lightly floured surface to a 10 inch (25.5 cm) round. Transfer this to the tin and, using your fingers, gradually ease the pastry up the side of the tin so that it stands up about ¼ inch (5 mm) above the edge all round.

Next, for the filling, mix the cranberry sauce or jelly with the lemon juice and spoon it on to the pastry, smoothing it out evenly to the edge. Use the rest of the dough to make a lattice-work pattern on the top, with strips about ¼ inch (5 mm) wide. Then go round the pastry edge with a fork, turning it over inside the edge of the tin to give about a ½ inch (1 cm) border all round. Place the tin on the pre-heated baking tray and bake on a high shelf for 30 minutes, or until the pastry is golden brown. Sift icing sugar over the top and serve the torte warm or cold with whipped cream.

Canadian Buttermilk Pancakes with Maple Syrup
Makes about 6

4 fl oz (120 ml) buttermilk

5 oz (150 g) plain flour

½ teaspoon baking powder

a pinch of salt

3 large eggs, beaten

about 1-2 oz (25-50 g) pure lard

To serve

lots of pure maple syrup and crème fraîche

Canada is where this profoundly unique syrup made from the sap of maple trees is made, and these are the pancakes that a certain Madame Lafond made for me when I was in Quebec; delightfully easy but tasting so light and fluffy. I love the way they puff up, crinkle and get really crisp at the edges. Serve these, as she did, straight from the pan on to warm plates, then absolutely drench them with maple syrup and add a generous dollop of crème fraîche.

First, sieve the flour, baking powder and salt together in a roomy bowl and make a well in the centre. After that, whisk the buttermilk and 3 fl oz (75 ml) cold water together in a jug and gradually whisk this into the bowl, slowly incorporating the flour with each new addition of liquid. Finally, add the eggs a little at a time until you have a smooth batter.

Now place a large, solid frying pan over a medium heat, add 2 teaspoons of the lard and heat it until the fat shimmers. Then, using a tablespoon of batter per pancake, place 2 or 3 spoonfuls into the pan.

They will take about 1 minute to turn golden brown, then turn them over, using a spatula and fork, and being careful not to splash yourself with the hot fat. Give them another 45 seconds on the other side, by which time they should have puffed up like little soufflés, then briefly rest them on some kitchen paper to absorb any excess fat.

Repeat this with the rest of the batter, adding a little more lard, if necessary. They will keep warm in a low oven, but to enjoy them at their best, have everyone seated to eat them as soon as they come out of the pan.

Apricot Galettes with Amaretto and Prune and Apple Galettes
Serves 6

For the pastry

4 oz (110 g) butter

6 oz (175 g) plain flour, plus a little flour for dusting

a pinch of salt

For the apricot galettes with Amaretto

27 ready-to-eat dried apricots or fresh apricots

6 teaspoons Amaretto liqueur

18 whole blanched almonds, toasted and cut into slivers (optional)

6 heaped teaspoons demerara sugar

a little icing sugar, sieved, to serve

For the prune and apple galettes

12 mi-cuit or pitted, dried Agen prunes, halved lengthways

3 small Cox's apples, unpeeled

a little ground cinnamon

2 tablespoons runny honey

You will also need two 10 x 12 inch (25.5 x 30 cm) solid baking sheets, lightly greased, and a 4 inch (10 cm) plain pastry cutter.

Galettes are very thin discs of flaky pastry, which, unlike conventional tarts, have no sides. The concept is a good one because the pastry is barely there, yet it gives a light, very crisp background to all kinds of toppings. Serve them with chilled crème fraîche or cream.

First of all, make the pastry. Remove a pack of butter from the fridge, weigh out 4 oz (110 g), then wrap it in a piece of foil and return it to the freezer or freezing compartment of the fridge for 30-45 minutes. Then, when you are ready to make the pastry, sift the flour and pinch of salt into a large, roomy bowl. Take the butter out of the freezer, fold back the foil and hold it in the foil, which will protect it from your warm hands. Then, using the coarse side of a grater placed in the bowl over the flour, grate the butter, dipping the edge of the butter into the flour several times to make it easier to grate. What you will end up with is a large pile of grated butter sitting in the middle of the flour. Now take a palette knife and start to distribute the gratings into the flour – don't use your hands yet, just keep trying to coat all the pieces of fat with flour. Then sprinkle 2 tablespoons of cold water all over, continue to use the palette knife to bring the whole thing together, and finish off, using your hands. If you need more moisture, that's fine – just remember that the dough should come together in such a way that it leaves the bowl fairly clean with no bits of loose butter or flour anywhere. Now pop it into a polythene bag and chill for 30 minutes before using.

Then roll the pastry out on a lightly floured surface to $\frac{1}{8}$ inch (3 mm), cut out six 4 inch (10 cm) discs and place these on the baking sheets. Meanwhile, pre-heat the oven to gas mark 7, 425°F (220°C).

If you are making the apricot galettes with Amaretto, cut the apricots in half and, if you are using fresh ones, remove the stones, then place 9 apricot halves on each round of pastry, topped by a few almond slivers (if using). Sprinkle a teaspoon of Amaretto over each one, then sprinkle them all with the demerara sugar. Bake for 10-12 minutes in the oven, one tray on the highest shelf, the other on the next one down, until the pastry is crisp and brown and the apricots have browned and caramelised a little at the edges, swapping the baking sheets over halfway through. Serve the galettes straight from the oven, sprinkled with icing sugar.

If you are making the prune and apple galettes, cut each apple into quarters, core and then cut each quarter into 2. Then arrange 4 prune halves and 4 slices of apple in a circle on top of each pastry round, then sprinkle over a little ground cinnamon. Now place the baking sheets in the oven for 10-12 minutes, one tray on the highest shelf, the other on the next one down, until the galettes are golden brown, swapping them over halfway through. Remove from the oven and, while they are still warm, glaze each one by brushing a little of the runny honey over the prunes and apples.

Fromage Frais Cheesecake with Strawberry Sauce
Serves 8

For the base

6 oz (175 g) sweet oat biscuits

2 oz (50 g) butter, melted

2 oz (50 g) coarsely chopped toasted hazelnuts

For the filling

12 oz (350 g) full-fat curd cheese

12 oz (350 g) fromage frais (8 per cent fat)

3 medium eggs

6 oz (175 g) golden caster sugar

1 teaspoon pure vanilla extract

For the topping

1 lb 8 oz (700 g) strawberries, hulled

2 tablespoons golden caster sugar

You will also need a springform cake tin, 9 inches (23 cm) in diameter, lightly buttered.

Pre-heat the oven to gas mark 2, 300°F (150°C).

Whenever I see cheesecake on a menu I'm filled with longing – there's something awfully comforting about cheesecake – but the question always arises as to whether it will or will not be cloying (and, if it is, what a waste of calories!). This version is definitely not cloying; It's light in texture and, made with fromage frais, a bit lighter on the calories, too.

Begin by crushing the biscuits in a food processor, or put them in a polythene bag, lay them flat, and then roll them with a rolling pin to crush them, then mix them with the melted butter and stir in the hazelnuts. Now press the mixture into the base of the tin and pop it into the fridge to firm up while the filling is made.

For this, combine in a large bowl the curd cheese, fromage frais, eggs, sugar and vanilla, using an electric hand whisk to beat everything together until silky smooth. Now pour this mixture over the biscuit base and place on the centre shelf of the oven to cook for 30 minutes. At the end of the cooking time turn off the oven but leave the cheesecake in the cooling oven to set until it's completely cold (I find that this is the best method as it prevents cracking). Remove the cheesecake from the oven and from the tin, transfer it to a plate, cover and chill till needed.

For the topping, weigh 8 oz (225 g) of the strawberries into a bowl, sprinkle them with the caster sugar and leave to soak for 30 minutes. After that, pile the strawberries and the sugar into a food processor and purée, then pass the purée through a nylon sieve to remove the seeds. To serve the cheesecake, arrange the remaining strawberries all over the surface, then spoon some of the purée over them and hand the rest of the purée round separately.

Gooseberry Crème Fraîche Tart
Serves 8

For the pastry

5 oz (150 g) plain flour, plus a little extra for rolling out

a pinch of salt

1¼ oz (30 g) softened butter, cut into smallish lumps

1¼ oz (30 g) softened pure lard, cut into smallish lumps

a little egg white (reserved from the filling)

For the filling

1 lb (450 g) gooseberries, topped and tailed

3½ fl oz (100 ml) crème fraîche

2 large egg yolks (reserve a little egg white for the pastry)

1½ oz (40 g) golden caster sugar

1 teaspoon balsamic vinegar

You will also need a 9 inch (23 cm), loose-based, fluted tart tin, 1 inch (2.5 cm) deep, lightly greased, and a solid baking sheet.

This one disappeared in seconds when we were developing the recipe. It's simple – just thin, crispy pastry and a layer of gooseberries set in custard. Delicious with or without some thick, yellow Jersey cream.

First of all, make the pastry. Sift the flour and pinch of salt into a bowl from a height to ensure it gets a good airing. Then take a knife and begin to cut the fats into the flour. Go on doing this until it looks fairly evenly blended, then rub in the fats, using your fingertips only and with as light a touch as possible. As you do so, lift it up high and let it fall back into the bowl, which means that all the time air is being incorporated – and air is what makes pastry light. Speed is what's needed here, so don't go on rubbing all day – just long enough to make the mixture crumbly, with a few odd lumps here and there.

Next, sprinkle a tablespoon of water over the mixture, then start bringing the dough together, using the knife to make it cling. Now discard the knife and finally, bring it together with your fingertips. When enough liquid is added, the pastry should leave the bowl completely clean. If this hasn't happened, then keep adding a spot more. (Sometimes it only needs your fingers dipped into water.) Place the pastry in a polythene bag and rest it in the fridge for about 30 minutes. Meanwhile, pre-heat the oven to gas mark 5, 375°F (190°C) and pre-heat the baking sheet at the same time.

Next, transfer the pastry to a flat, lightly floured surface and roll it out to a circle the diameter of the tin. Line the tin with the pastry, press it up about ¼ inch (5 mm) above the rim of the tin all round, then prick the base all over with a fork. Now brush the base and sides with some of the egg white left over from the eggs for the filling. After that, place the pastry-lined tin on the hot baking sheet and bake for 20 minutes until the pastry is just beginning to turn golden. Then remove it and reduce the heat to gas mark 4, 350°F (180°C).

Next, whisk the crème fraîche, yolks, sugar and vinegar together for the filling. Arrange the gooseberries in the pastry case, pour the crème fraîche mixture over them and return the tart to the oven for 40-45 minutes, or until it is a light golden brown. Then remove it from the oven and allow it to settle for about 20 minutes before serving. It also tastes extremely good served cold.

Lemon Ricotta Cheesecake with a Confit of Lemons
Serves 6

For the confit of lemons

2 large juicy lemons (unwaxed if possible)

4 oz (110 g) granulated sugar

For the base

4 oz (110 g) sweet oat biscuits

1 oz (25 g) ready-toasted flaked almonds

2 oz (50 g) melted butter

For the filling

3-4 lemons

12 oz (350 g) ricotta cheese

1 x 11.7 g sachet powdered gelatine

2 large egg yolks

2½ oz (60 g) golden caster sugar

10 fl oz (275 ml) double cream

You will also need a 7 inch (18 cm) or 8 inch (20 cm) springform cake tin – line the sides with baking parchment to come 1 inch (2.5 cm) above the rim – a non-aluminium pan, about 8 inches (20 cm) in diameter, and a circle of baking parchment of the same diameter.

This is a very light, fluffy lemony cheesecake, which, if you serve it with a confit of lemons, makes a delightfully refreshing end to a rich meal.

Start by making the confit as this needs to be prepared ahead of time – the day before you want to serve it, if possible. Take 1½ of the lemons and slice them into thin rings about ⅛ inch (3 mm) thick, discarding the end pieces and pips. Place these in the non-aluminium saucepan and cover with sufficient cold water to just cover them, bring to a simmer for 3 minutes, then drain through a sieve and discard the water. Now pour 12 fl oz (340 ml) water into the same pan, add the sugar, stir over a gentle heat until all the grains have dissolved, then add the lemon slices. Once the liquid has returned to a very gentle simmer lay the circle of baking parchment on the surface of the liquid – this will help the lemon slices to cook evenly.

Now continue to cook them at the very gentlest simmer, without a lid, for 45 minutes – until the skins are tender. Check them at 30 minutes by inserting the tip of a knife just in case they are cooking a little faster. When they are tender, remove them with a slotted spoon to a shallow dish. The liquid will be much reduced at this stage, but what you want is about 5 fl oz (150 ml); if you have much more than this, increase the heat a little and reduce further. Then squeeze the juice from the remaining ½ lemon, pour it into the syrup and pour this over the lemon slices. Cover and leave overnight if possible.

To make the cheesecake, first of all, pre-heat the oven to gas mark 6, 400°F (200°C), then prepare the base by crushing the biscuits – the best way to do this is to lay them flat inside a polythene bag then roll them with a rolling pin to crush them coarsely. Then tip them into a bowl, along with the flaked almonds, and stir the melted butter into them. After that, press this mixture evenly and firmly on to the base of the cake tin and then place in the oven to pre-bake for 20 minutes. After that, remove it from the oven and allow it to get completely cold.

Meanwhile, remove the zest from 3 of the lemons, using a fine grater (it can be grated on to a board and chopped even more finely, if required). Then squeeze enough juice from the lemons to measure 5 fl oz (150 ml). Next, put 3 tablespoons of the lemon juice into a small bowl, sprinkle the gelatine over, then place the bowl in a small saucepan with 1 inch (2.5 cm) simmering water and leave it for 10 minutes to dissolve, or until it is absolutely clear and transparent.

Now put the egg yolks, sugar and ricotta cheese into a food processor or liquidiser and blend it all on a high speed for about 1 minute. Then add the lemon zest, remaining lemon juice and the gelatine, which should be poured through a strainer. Blend everything again now until it's all absolutely smooth. Then take a large bowl and whisk the double cream until you get a floppy consistency, then pour this in to join the rest of the cheese mixture and blend again, this time for just a few seconds. Next, pour the whole lot over the biscuit base, cover with foil and chill in the fridge for a minimum of 3 hours.

To serve the cheesecake, carefully remove it from the tin on to a serving plate, decorate with a circle of lemon confit slices and serve the rest separately.

Note This recipe contains raw eggs.

Lemon Ricotta Cheesecake
with a Confit of Lemons

Eighteenth-century Creamed Apple Flan
Serves 6

For the pastry

1 oz (25 g) softened butter, cut into smallish lumps

1 oz (25 g) softened pure lard

4 oz (110 g) plain flour, sifted, plus a little extra for rolling out

For the filling

4 large Bramley cooking apples, peeled, cored and sliced

3 digestive biscuits

2 oz (50 g) butter

2 tablespoons golden caster sugar

grated zest of 1 small lemon

2 tablespoons brandy or cider

whole nutmeg for grating

3 large egg yolks

2½ fl oz (65 ml) double cream

To serve

icing sugar, to dust

You will also need a loose-based, fluted tart tin 8 inches (20 cm) in diameter, 1¼ inches (3 cm) deep, lightly greased.

Pre-heat the oven to gas mark 4, 350°F (180°C).

This recipe is a nostalgic one for me as it's one of the first I tried after some research into eighteenth-century British cooking at the British Museum, and it prompted me to do a whole lot more.

Make up the pastry by rubbing the fats into the sifted flour until the mixture resembles breadcrumbs. Then add 1-2 teaspoons of water to make a dough that leaves the bowl clean. Pop the pastry into a polythene bag and leave to rest in the fridge for 30 minutes or so, then roll it out on a lightly floured surface and use to line the tart tin. Prick the base all over with a fork, and bake for 20 minutes.

Meanwhile, put the sliced apples in a saucepan with 2 tablespoons of water and cook until they are pulpy. Transfer them to a large mixing bowl and beat until you have a smooth purée.

Now crush the biscuits – the best way to do this is to lay them flat inside a polythene bag then roll them with a rolling pin to crush them into crumbs.

Whisk the butter and the caster sugar into the apple purée, followed by the biscuit crumbs, lemon zest, brandy or cider and a good grating of nutmeg. Combine everything thoroughly and leave the mixture to cool.

Next, whisk the egg yolks together with the cream – don't overdo it, you just want to thicken it slightly. Then, when the apple mixture has cooled, stir the egg yolks and cream into it. Pour the whole lot into the partly cooked flan case, then bake in the oven for a further 30 minutes. Allow to cool, and serve, dusted with icing sugar.

Poached Pear Galettes
Serves 6

For the pastry

4 oz (110 g) butter

6 oz (175 g) plain flour, plus a little extra for dusting

a pinch of salt

For the poached pear galettes

3 firm unripe pears, peeled but with the stalks left on

10 fl oz (275 ml) red wine

1 oz (25 g) golden caster sugar

½ cinnamon stick

½ vanilla pod

1 teaspoon arrowroot

You will also need two 10 x 12 inch (25.5 x 30 cm) solid baking sheets, lightly greased, and a 4 inch (10 cm) plain pastry cutter.

These are exceptionally pretty to look at, and I like to serve them as a sweet ending to a special meal. They are a bit more trouble than the galettes on page 86 but still very easy to make and assemble.

First of all, make the pastry. Remove a pack of butter from the fridge, weigh out 4 oz (110 g), then wrap it in a piece of foil and return it to the freezer or freezing compartment of the fridge for 30-45 minutes. Then, when you are ready to make the pastry, sift the flour and a pinch of salt into a large, roomy bowl. Take the butter out of the freezer, fold back the foil and hold it in the foil, which will protect it from your warm hands. Then, using the coarse side of a grater placed in the bowl over the flour, grate the butter, dipping the edge of the butter into the flour several times to make it easier to grate. What you will end up with is a large pile of grated butter sitting in the middle of the flour. Now take a palette knife and start to distribute the gratings into the flour – don't use your hands yet, just keep trying to coat all the pieces of fat with flour. Then sprinkle 2 tablespoons of cold water all over, continue to use the palette knife to bring the whole thing together, and finish off, using your hands. If you need more moisture, that's fine – just remember that the dough should come together in such a way that it leaves the bowl fairly clean, with no bits of loose butter or flour anywhere. Now pop it into a polythene bag and chill for 30 minutes in the fridge.

Meanwhile, find a lidded saucepan that will fit the pears comfortably, laying them in the pan on their sides. Now mix the wine with the sugar and pour this over the pears, then add the cinnamon stick and vanilla pod. Put the lid on the pan and gently simmer the pears for 45 minutes until tender when tested with a skewer. Turn them over halfway through the cooking time so the other half sits in the wine and they colour evenly. Towards the end of the cooking time, pre-heat the oven to gas mark 7, 425°F (220°C). Then roll the pastry out on a lightly floured surface to ⅛ inch (3 mm), cut out six 4 inch (10 cm) discs and place these on the baking sheets.

Now lift the pears from the liquid and halve them by first making a slit in the stalk as you press it on to a flat surface. Then stand each pear upright and cut through the split stalk, halve the pears and remove the cores. Now you need to slice each half into a fan, so take a sharp knife and, starting from the top of the stalk end, about ½ inch (1 cm) in, slice the pear downwards and at a slight angle so you end up with the slices of pear fanning out but still attached to the stalk.

Now place each half pear on to a pastry base and fan it out, then place the baking sheets in the oven for 10-12 minutes, one on the top shelf, the other on the next one down, swapping them over halfway through the cooking time.

Meanwhile, you need to reduce the poaching liquid, so first remove the cinnamon stick and vanilla pod, and place the saucepan over a high heat and let the liquid bubble for about 5 minutes. Then, in a cup, mix the arrowroot with a little cold water until you have a smooth paste, and add this to the saucepan, whisking with a balloon whisk all the time. This will thicken the sauce slightly. Now remove it from the heat and leave it to cool.

When the tarts are ready, remove them from the oven. Serve hot or cold, but just before serving, pour a little of the syrup over each tart to give them a pretty glaze.

Creams Jellies Meringues Fruit

Coffee Cappuccino Creams with Cream and Sweet Coffee Sauce
Serves 6

For the creams

6 heaped teaspoons instant espresso coffee powder

1 x 11.7 g sachet powdered gelatine

10 fl oz (275 ml) whole milk

3 large eggs, separated

1 rounded teaspoon cornflour

7 fl oz (200 ml) crème fraîche

5 fl oz (150 ml) double cream, to serve

For the sauce

3 heaped teaspoons instant espresso coffee powder

6 oz (175 g) golden granulated sugar

You will also need six 7 fl oz (200 ml) serving glasses.

If you are a coffee fan, this is *the* coffee dessert – the best ever! It is based on an old-fashioned recipe for honeycomb mould, which sometimes separates into layers but sadly, often doesn't. Therefore, I have now given up on layers because, anyway, it tastes absolutely divine. You can make this and serve it in Irish coffee glasses or plain glasses. The contrast of the unsweetened coffee cream mingling with the sweetened sauce and a generous amount of pouring or whipping cream is just gorgeous.

Begin by soaking the gelatine: pour 5 fl oz (150 ml) of water into a small bowl, sprinkle in the gelatine and let it soak for 5 minutes. Meanwhile, pour the milk into a medium saucepan and place it over a gentle heat. Then, in a bowl, whisk the egg yolks and cornflour together and, when the milk is very hot and just about to simmer, pour it over the egg yolk mixture, whisking as you do. Now return the whole lot to the same saucepan, adding the soaked gelatine and coffee powder, then return the pan to the heat and continue to whisk until the custard is thickened and the gelatine and coffee are completely dissolved. Remove the pan from the heat and pour the custard into a large mixing bowl, leave it to cool, then whisk in the crème fraîche.

In another bowl, and using a clean whisk, whisk the egg whites to the soft-peak stage. Now fold 2 tablespoons of the egg whites into the coffee custard to loosen the mixture, then gently fold in the rest. Pour the mixture into the glasses and leave, covered with clingfilm, in a cool place for about 2 hours, then chill in the fridge until needed.

To make the coffee sauce, gently heat the sugar and 8 fl oz (225 ml) of water together and whisk till all the sugar granules have completely dissolved, then simmer gently for 15 minutes without a lid, until it becomes syrupy. Next, dissolve the coffee in 1 dessertspoon of warm water, stir this into the syrup and transfer it to a serving jug to cool. Meanwhile, whip up the double cream to the floppy stage and, when you're ready, serve the coffee creams topped with whipped cream and the coffee syrup poured over.

Note This recipe contains raw eggs.

Old-fashioned Rhubarb Trifle
Serves 6

1 lb 8 oz (700 g) rhubarb

4 oz (110 g) golden caster sugar, plus a little extra, if needed

grated zest and juice of 1 orange

2 oz (50 g) pecan nuts

6 trifle sponges

3 tablespoons marmalade

4 fl oz (120 ml) sercial (dry) Madeira

about 10 fl oz (275 ml) freshly squeezed orange juice

1 x 11.7 g sachet powdered gelatine

12 oz (350 g) fresh custard

7 oz (200 g) Greek yoghurt

You will also need an ovenproof baking dish, 7½ inches (19 cm) square, and 2 inches (5 cm) deep, and 6 individual serving bowls, or a large trifle bowl with a capacity of 3½ pints (2 litres).

Pre-heat the oven to gas mark 4, 350°F (180°C).

Old-fashioned because when I was a child – a very long time ago – I used to love jelly trifles, and my mother would always make one for my birthday. This is a much more adult version, and the sharp, fragrant acidity of the rhubarb makes it a very light and refreshing dessert for spring and early summer.

To prepare the rhubarb, cut it into 1 inch (2.5 cm) chunks and add these to the baking dish. Then sprinkle in the caster sugar, together with the zest and juice of the orange. Now pop the whole lot in the oven, without covering, and let it cook for 30-40 minutes, until the rhubarb is tender but still retains its shape. At the same time, place the pecans in the oven and put a timer on for 7 minutes to toast them lightly, then you can either leave them whole or chop them roughly. While the rhubarb is cooking, slice the trifle sponges in half lengthways, spread each half with the marmalade, then re-form them and cut each one into 3 little sandwiches. Now arrange them either in the individual serving bowls or the large trifle bowl. Then make a few stabs in the sponges and sprinkle the Madeira carefully over them, then leave it all aside so it can soak in.

When the rhubarb is cooked and has become completely cold, taste it – if it is a bit sharp, add a little more sugar. Take a draining spoon and carefully remove the chunks of rhubarb, placing them in and among the sponges. Now pour all the juices from the dish into a measuring jug and make this up to 18 fl oz (510 ml) with the orange juice.

Next, pour 8 fl oz (225 ml) of this into a small saucepan, scatter the gelatine over, whisk it and leave it to soak for 5 minutes. Then place the pan over a gentle heat and whisk everything until all the gelatine has completely dissolved – about 2 minutes – then return this to the remaining juice in the jug and give it all another good whisk. Now pour it over the sponges and rhubarb. When it is completely cold, cover it with clingfilm and leave in the fridge till completely set. The last thing you need to do is whisk the custard and Greek yoghurt together in a mixing bowl, then spoon this mixture over the set jelly. Now cover with clingfilm again and chill until you're ready to serve. Don't forget to sprinkle the toasted pecan nuts over just before serving, and, although it doesn't strictly need it, a little chilled pouring cream is a nice addition.

Apricot Hazelnut Meringue
Serves 6

For the meringue

3 oz (75 g) ground hazelnuts

3 large egg whites

6 oz (175 g) white caster sugar

For the filling

4 oz (110 g) dried apricots, soaked overnight in water

juice of 1 small orange

1 small strip orange peel

½ inch (1 cm) cinnamon stick

1 tablespoon light soft brown sugar

2 teaspoons arrowroot

To finish

10 fl oz (275 ml) double cream

a few whole toasted hazelnuts

You will also need 2 sponge tins, 7 inches (18 cm) in diameter, 1½ inches (4 cm) deep, lightly oiled, and the bases lined with baking parchment.

Pre-heat the oven to gas mark 5, 375°F (190°C).

A light and delicious – and rather special – sweet. The sharpness of the apricots counter-acts the sweetness of the meringue, which has a lovely nutty flavour. You can buy ready-ground hazelnuts at wholefood shops and delicatessens, or if you're grinding your own, brown them first in the oven at gas mark 4, 350°F (180°C) for 10 minutes and grind them in a food processor or liquidiser.

First, whisk the egg whites in a large, scrupulously clean bowl until they form stiff peaks, then whisk in the caster sugar, a little at a time. Then, using a large metal spoon, lightly fold in the ground hazelnuts. Now divide the mixture equally between the 2 tins and level them out. Bake the meringues on the centre shelf of the oven for 20-30 minutes. Leave them in the tins to cool for 30 minutes before turning them out (the surface will look uneven, but don't worry). Then loosen round the edges, turn the meringues out on to a cooling rack and strip off the base papers.

While the meringues are cooking, you can prepare the apricot filling. Drain the soaked apricots in a sieve over a bowl, then transfer the apricots to a small saucepan and add the orange juice, peel, cinnamon stick and sugar, plus 2 tablespoons of the soaking water. Simmer gently for 10-15 minutes until they are tender when tested with a skewer, then remove the cinnamon stick and orange peel. Mix the arrowroot with a little cold water and add this to the apricot mixture, stirring over a fairly low heat, until the mixture has thickened. Then leave it to get quite cold.

To serve the meringue: whip the cream, then carefully spread the cold apricot mixture over one meringue, followed by half the whipped cream. Place the other meringue on top, spread the remaining cream over that and decorate the top with some whole toasted hazelnuts.

Summer Fruit Compote
Serves 6

3 peaches

6 apricots

6 large plums

8 oz (225 g) blueberries

6 oz (175 g) raspberries

2 oz (50 g) golden caster sugar, plus a little extra, if needed

You will also need a shallow baking dish: I use a round dish approximately 12 inches (30 cm) in diameter.

Pre-heat the oven to gas mark 4, 350°F (180°C).

Any mixture of fruit can be used for this, but remember the flavour of blackcurrants does tend to dominate – so, if you're using them, just use a half-quantity compared with the other fruits. If you want to make the compote entirely with soft berries, it needs only 10 minutes in the oven.

First, prepare the fruit. Halve each peach by making a slit all round through the natural crease, then simply twist in half and remove the stone. Cut the halves into 3 pieces each and place them in the baking dish. After that, do the same with the apricots and, if they're large, slice the halves into 2; if they're small, leave the halves whole. Repeat this with the plums, but if they're clinging too tightly to their stones you may find it easier to slice them into quarters on the stone and pull each quarter off.

Add the apricots and plums to the peaches in the dish, followed by the blueberries. Now sprinkle the sugar over them, place the dish in the centre of the oven and let the fruits bake, without covering, for 25-30 minutes or until they are tender when tested with a skewer and the juices have run. Then remove them from the oven and gently stir in the raspberries, tipping the dish and basting them with the hot juices. Taste to check the sugar and add more if you think it needs it, then cool the compote and chill in the fridge. Serve with crème fraîche, or this is wonderful with ice cream.

Pink Champagne Jellies with Champagne Cream
Serves 6

10 fl oz (275 ml) pink Champagne, plus about 6 tablespoons for the Champagne cream

5 sheets leaf gelatine

1 large lemon

3 oz (75 g) golden caster sugar

5 fl oz (150 ml) double cream, softly whipped

You will also need 6 martini glasses with a 5 fl oz (150 ml) capacity or similar.

This is a tried and trusted recipe and one of my personal favourites. The Champagne cream is best made at the last minute, with Champagne from a freshly opened bottle – it's a great experience actually eating it with all the bubbles in it, and you can always drink the rest of the Champagne!

To make the jelly, first soak the leaves of gelatine in a bowl of cold water until soft (about 5 minutes). Next, measure 15 fl oz (425 ml) of water into a saucepan, scrub the lemon then, using a peeler, pare off the coloured part only of the zest, add this to the pan, along with the sugar, and bring up to simmering point.

After that, take the pan off the heat, squeeze the leaves of gelatine with your hand to remove the excess water and add them to the hot lemon and water mixture, whisking all the time with a balloon whisk until the gelatine has melted. Add the juice of the lemon, then strain the contents of the pan into a large bowl either through a coffee filter or a fine sieve lined with muslin or gauze. Leave to cool, then cover and chill in the fridge until the jelly is on the point of setting. This should take about 1-1½ hours.

After that, uncork the Champagne, measure out 10 fl oz (275 ml) and pour it into the jelly, stirring once or twice to blend everything together. Then ladle the jelly gently into serving glasses, trying to conserve as many bubbles as you can so they will be apparent when the jelly is eaten. Chill the jellies, covered with clingfilm, for 4 hours, by which time they should be deliciously soft set.

For the cream, no real measurement here, I'm afraid, because the Champagne has to be poured straight from the bottle and whisked into the cream – but we have calculated that 6 guessed tablespoons is about right for 5 fl oz (150 ml) of softly whipped double cream.

Note If you'd prefer to use powdered gelatine instead of leaf, sprinkle the contents of an 11.7 g sachet over 2 tablespoons of water in a small heatproof bowl, placed in a saucepan of simmering water. Remove the pan from the heat and leave to stand for 10 minutes. Whisk into the hot lemon and water mixture as above.

Vanilla Cream Terrine with Raspberries and Blackcurrant Coulis
Serves 6

For the terrine

2 teaspoons pure vanilla extract

15 fl oz (425 ml) whipping cream

1 x 11.7 g sachet powdered gelatine

3 oz (75 g) golden caster sugar

15 fl oz (425 ml) Greek yoghurt

For the blackcurrant coulis

8 oz (225 g) blackcurrants

3 oz (75 g) golden caster sugar, plus a little extra, if needed

To garnish

6 oz (175 g) raspberries

fresh mint leaves

You will also need a plastic box, 4 x 4 x 4 inches (10 x 10 x 10 cm).

This is one of those oh-so-simple-but-oh-so-good desserts that offers precisely the right background to vivid, rich fruit like blackcurrants.

Begin by placing the gelatine in a cup, together with 3 tablespoons of the cream, and leave it to soak for 10 minutes. Meanwhile, place the rest of the cream in a saucepan with the sugar and heat gently till the sugar has dissolved (it's important not to over-heat the cream). Next, add the soaked gelatine to the warm cream and whisk everything over the heat for a few seconds. Now remove the cream mixture from the heat.

In a mixing bowl, stir the yoghurt and vanilla together, then pour in the gelatine cream mixture through a sieve. Mix very thoroughly and pour the whole lot into the plastic box, allow to cool, then cover and chill in the fridge for at least 4-6 hours, or preferably overnight, until it's set.

Meanwhile, make the blackcurrant coulis by first de-stalking the blackcurrants (see Summer Pudding, page 122) and then sprinkling them with the sugar in a bowl. Leave to soak for 30 minutes, and then you can either sieve them directly back into the bowl or, to make the sieving easier, whiz them first in a food processor, then sieve into the bowl. Taste to check that you have added enough sugar, then pour into a jug and chill until you're ready to serve the terrine.

To serve, turn the terrine out on to a board, first sliding a palette knife around the edges to loosen it, then giving it a hefty shake. Then cut into 6 slices. Arrange each slice on a serving plate, spoon a little blackcurrant coulis over the opposite corners of each one and decorate with the fresh raspberries and mint leaves.

A Terrine of Summer Fruits
Serves 8

15 fl oz (425 ml) sparkling rosé wine

2 oz (50 g) golden caster sugar

2 x 11.7 g sachets powdered gelatine

1 tablespoon fresh lime juice

For the fruit

12 oz (350 g) small strawberries

8 oz (225 g) raspberries

12 oz (350 g) blackcurrants, redcurrants and blueberries – 4 oz (110 g) of each or any other combination you like

You will also need 2 non-stick 2 lb (900 g) loaf tins, 4¾ x 7½ inches (12 x 19 cm) and 3½ inches (9 cm) deep.

This one is a stunner. It's also dead easy to make and slices like a dream – a lovely, fresh-tasting, summer dessert. It's important to have two tins because the terrine needs to be weighted while it is setting. In testing, I have found that it is necessary to add the smaller amount of jelly at the end to avoid spillage when weighting, as it's this weighting that makes the terrine easy to slice.

First, prepare the fruit: remove the stalks and halve the strawberries if they are any larger than a quail's egg. Then mix the fruits together in a large bowl, being very gentle so as to avoid bruising them.

In a small saucepan, heat half the rosé wine till it begins to simmer, then whisk the sugar and gelatine into it. Make sure that everything has dissolved completely before adding the remaining wine and the lime juice. Then pour the liquid into a jug and allow it to cool. While that's happening, lay the mixed fruit in one of the loaf tins – and it's worth arranging the bottom layer with the smallest, prettiest-shaped fruit as this will be on top when the terrine is turned out.

Next, pour all but 5 fl oz (150 ml) of the liquid over the fruit. Now lay a sheet of clingfilm over the tin, place the other tin directly on top, then put 2 unopened tins of tomatoes or something similar to act as weights into the top tin and put the whole lot into the fridge for about 1 hour, or until it has set. Then warm up the remaining 5 fl oz (150 ml) of the wine mixture and pour it over the surface of the terrine. Re-cover with clingfilm and return to the fridge overnight to set firm.

When you are ready to serve, turn out the terrine by dipping the tin very briefly in hot water and inverting it on to a plate. Use a very sharp knife (also dipped first into hot water) to cut it into slices. Serve with chilled pouring cream, crème fraîche or Greek yoghurt.

A Terrine of Summer Fruits

Crème Caramel
Serves 4-6

5 fl oz (150 ml) milk

10 fl oz (275 ml) single cream

4 large eggs

1½ oz (40 g) soft brown sugar

a few drops of pure vanilla extract

For the caramel

4 oz (110 g) granulated
or caster sugar

You will also need a soufflé dish
with a capacity of 1½ pints
(850 ml), 5 inches (13 cm) in
diameter, 3 inches (7.5 cm) deep,
and a large, deep roasting tin.

Pre-heat the oven to gas mark 2,
300°F (150°C).

My husband Michael always makes this at home. It turns out in a pool of lovely dark toffee caramel, and is soft and creamy within. If you are feeling really wicked, serve with some chilled Jersey pouring cream – ecstasy!

First, make the caramel. Put the granulated or caster sugar in a medium saucepan over a medium heat. When the sugar begins to melt, bubble and darken, stir and continue to cook until it has become a uniform liquid syrup, about two or three shades darker than golden syrup. Take the pan off the heat and cautiously add 2 tablespoons of tap-hot water – it will splutter and bubble quite considerably but will soon subside. Stir and, when the syrup is once again smooth, quickly pour it into the base of the dish, tipping it around to coat the sides a little.

Now pour the milk and cream into another pan and leave it to heat gently while you whisk together the eggs, brown sugar and a few drops of vanilla extract in a large bowl. Then, when the milk and cream are steaming hot, pour on to the egg and sugar mixture, whisking until thoroughly blended. Then pour the liquid into the dish and place it in the roasting tin. Transfer the tin carefully to the oven, then pour hot water into it to surround the dish up to two-thirds in depth. Bake for 1 hour. Cool and chill the crème caramel. Remove from the fridge 1 hour before you're ready to serve it. Free the edges by running a knife around before inverting it on to a serving plate.

Petits Monts Blancs
Serves 8

For the meringues

2 large egg whites

4 oz (110 g) white caster sugar

For the filling

2 x 250 g tins crème de marrons de l'Ardèche (sweetened chestnut purée), chilled

For the mascarpone cream

9 oz (250 g) mascarpone

7 fl oz (200 ml) fromage frais (8 per cent fat)

1 rounded dessertspoon caster sugar

1 teaspoon pure vanilla extract

a little icing sugar for dusting

You will also need a 12 x 16 inch (30 x 40 cm) baking sheet, lined with baking parchment.

Pre-heat the oven to gas mark 2, 300°F (150°C).

When I first worked in a restaurant kitchen in the early 1960s, this recipe was on the menu and I became totally addicted to the sweetened chestnut purée. Chestnut has an amazing affinity with meringue and whipped cream, but in this modern version I have replaced the cream with mascarpone and fromage frais; this way you get the flavour and creamy richness of the mascarpone but lightened by the fromage frais. In the summer, soft fruit makes the perfect filling.

To make the meringues, place the egg whites in a large, spanking clean bowl and, using an electric hand whisk on a low speed, begin whisking. Continue for about 2 minutes, until the whites are foamy, then switch the speed to medium and carry on whisking for 1 more minute. Now turn the speed to high and continue whisking until the egg whites reach the stiff-peak stage. Next, whisk the sugar in on high, a little at a time (about a dessertspoon), until you have a stiff and glossy mixture.

Now all you do is spoon 8 heaped dessertspoons of the mixture on to the prepared baking sheet, spacing them evenly. Then, using the back of the spoon or a small palette knife, hollow out the centres. Don't worry if they are not all the same shape – random and rocky is how I would describe them.

Next, pop them on the centre shelf of the oven, immediately reduce the heat to gas mark 1, 275°F (140°C) and leave them for 30 minutes. After that, turn the oven off and leave the meringues to dry out in the warmth of the oven until it is completely cold (usually about 4 hours) or overnight. The meringues will store well in a tin or plastic box, and will even freeze extremely well.

To assemble the Monts Blancs, spoon equal quantities of the crème de marrons into each meringue, whisk the mascarpone cream ingredients together (except the icing sugar) and then spoon equal amounts on top of the chestnut purée. A light dusting of icing sugar is good for a snowcapped-mountain image.

Summer Pudding
Serves 6

8 oz (225 g) redcurrants

4 oz (110 g) blackcurrants

1 lb (450 g) raspberries

5 oz (150 g) golden caster sugar

7-8 medium slices white bread from a large loaf, crusts removed

You will also need a 1½ pint (850 ml) pudding basin.

Maybe the reason why this pudding is such a favourite is because we only have these particular fruits for such a short time each year – anyway, in our house it's become a sort of annual event. Do try to get a well-made white loaf though: the texture of sliced white is most unsuitable.

Separate the redcurrants and blackcurrants from their stalks by holding the tip of each stalk firmly between finger and thumb and sliding it between the prongs of a fork, pushing the fork downwards, so pulling off the berries as it goes. Rinse all the fruits, picking out any raspberries that look at all musty.

Place the fruits with the sugar in a large saucepan over a medium heat and let them cook for about 3-5 minutes, only until the sugar has dissolved and the juices begin to run – don't overcook and so spoil the fresh flavour. Now remove the fruit from the heat, and line the pudding basin with the slices of bread, overlapping them and sealing well by pressing the edges together. Fill in any gaps with small pieces of bread, so that no juice can get through when you add the fruit.

Pour the fruit and juice in (except for about two-thirds of a cupful), then cover the pudding with another slice of bread. Now place a small plate or saucer (one that will fit exactly inside the rim of the bowl) on top, and on top of that place a 3 lb or 4 lb (1.35 kg or 1.8 kg) scale weight. If you don't have weights, use any heavy object: a tin of food, or any other innovation you can think of. Leave the pudding in the fridge overnight.

Just before serving the pudding, turn it out on to a large serving dish and spoon the reserved juice all over, to soak any bits of bread that still look white. Serve, cut into wedges, with a bowl of thick cream on the table.

Gooseberry Yoghurt Fool
Serves 6

2 lb (900 g) gooseberries, topped and tailed with scissors

10 oz (275 g) Greek yoghurt

5 oz (150 g) golden caster sugar

sprigs of mint, to garnish

You will also need a shallow 9 inch (23 cm) square or round ovenproof baking dish, and 6 serving glasses, each with a capacity of 6 fl oz (175 ml).

Pre-heat the oven to gas mark 4, 350°F (180°C).

I now find that lusciously thick genuine Greek yoghurt makes the best fruit fool of all, as it allows the full flavour of the fruit to dominate. If you're serving this to someone who doesn't like yoghurt, don't worry – they won't know.

For the fullest flavour, I think gooseberries are best cooked in the oven. So first, place them in the baking dish, sprinkle in the sugar and bake them on the centre shelf of the oven, uncovered, for 20-30 minutes, or until tender when tested with a skewer. After that, tip them into a sieve set over a bowl to drain off the excess juice. Now reserve about a quarter of the cooked gooseberries for later, then place the rest in the bowl of a food processor, add 4 tablespoons of the reserved juice and whiz to a thick purée.

After that, leave the purée to get quite cold, then empty the yoghurt into a bowl, give it a stir, then fold in half the purée. Now spoon this mixture into the serving glasses, spoon the rest of the purée on top and, finally, add the reserved gooseberries. Cover the glasses with clingfilm and chill till you're ready to serve, then serve, garnished with sprigs of mint, and some small shortbreads.

VARIATION
Rhubarb Yoghurt Fool
Serves 4

For a delicious variation on the recipe above, trim and wash 1 lb 4 oz (570 g) of rhubarb and cut it into 1 inch (2.5 cm) chunks. Place in a baking dish, sprinkle with 3 oz (75 g) of golden caster sugar and add 1 teaspoon of chopped fresh root ginger, then cook in the oven, at the same temperature, for 30-40 minutes, until tender. Now drain the rhubarb as above, then purée all the rhubarb, along with 2 tablespoons of the reserved juice. When cool, fold half the purée into 7 fl oz (200 ml) of Greek yoghurt in a bowl, then divide it among 4 serving glasses and spoon the remaining purée on top. Finally, cut 2 pieces of stem ginger into matchstick lengths and use them to garnish the fool. Cover with clingfilm and refrigerate until needed.

Fromage Frais Creams with Red Fruit Compote
Serves 6

For the creams

1 lb 12 oz (800 g) fromage frais
(8 per cent fat)

3 sheets leaf gelatine

5 fl oz (150 ml) semi-skimmed milk

3 oz (75 g) golden caster sugar

1 vanilla pod, split lengthways

For the compote

8 oz (225 g) each plums,
cherries, blueberries,
strawberries, raspberries

2 oz (50 g) golden caster sugar

You will also need 6 mini pudding
basins, each with a capacity of
6 fl oz (175 ml), lightly oiled with a
flavourless oil, and an ovenproof
baking dish, 9 inches (23 cm)
square and 2 inches (5 cm) deep.

Pre-heat the oven to gas mark 4,
350°F (180°C).

I originally made these with mascarpone, but this low-fat alternative is, I feel, every bit as good as the rich version and the perfect accompaniment to any fruit compote. I like this best made with leaf gelatine, but I've also included instructions for powdered gelatine.

If you are using leaf gelatine, simply place the sheets in a bowl and cover with cold water, then leave them to soak for about 5 minutes, till softened.

Meanwhile, place the milk in a saucepan with the sugar and vanilla pod and heat gently for 5 minutes, or until the sugar has dissolved. Then take the pan off the heat and all you do now is squeeze the leaf gelatine in your hands to remove any excess water, then add it to the hot milk. Give it all a thorough whisking and leave to cool.

Next, in a large mixing bowl, whisk the fromage frais until smooth, then add the cooled gelatine and milk mixture, removing the vanilla pod, and whisk again really well. Now divide the mixture among the pudding basins, filling them to within ½ inch (1 cm) of the rims. Finally, cover with clingfilm and chill in the fridge for at least 3 hours.

To make the compote, begin by preparing the plums: cut them round their natural line into halves, remove the stones, then cut each half into 4 and place in the ovenproof dish, along with the whole cherries and blueberries. Now sprinkle in the sugar, then place the dish on the centre shelf of the oven without covering and leave it there for 15 minutes.

Next, stir in the strawberries, halved if large, and return the dish to the oven for 10-15 minutes, or until the fruits are tender and the juices have run out of them. Finally, remove them from the oven and stir the raspberries into the hot juices, then allow it to cool, cover with clingfilm and chill.

To serve the creams, gently ease each one away from the edge of the basin using your little finger, then invert them on to individual serving dishes and serve with the compote spooned all around.

If you'd prefer to use powdered gelatine instead of leaf, place 3 tablespoons of the milk in a small bowl, then sprinkle the contents of an 11.7 g sachet over the milk and leave it to stand for 5 minutes. Meanwhile, heat the rest of the milk in a small saucepan, along with the vanilla pod and sugar, until the sugar has dissolved, then remove it from the heat and whisk in the soaked gelatine mixture. Allow to cool, then just whisk into the fromage frais and continue as for the main recipe.

Tropical Fruit Salad in Planter's Punch
Serves 8

2 bananas, peeled and chopped into 1 inch (2.5 cm) chunks

8 oz (225 g) seedless black grapes, halved

1 pawpaw, peeled and chopped into 1 inch (2.5 cm) chunks

1 large mango, peeled and chopped into 1 inch (2.5 cm) chunks

1 small pineapple, peeled and chopped into 1 inch (2.5 cm) chunks

2 oranges, peeled and cut into segments

8 oz (225 g) lychees, peeled, stoned and halved

2 kiwi fruit, peeled, halved and cut into ½ inch (1 cm) slices

4 passion fruit, halved

whole nutmeg for grating

For the syrup

4 oz (110 g) golden granulated sugar

2 small cinnamon sticks

pared zest and juice of 2 limes

4 fl oz (120 ml) freshly squeezed orange juice

4 fl oz (120 ml) pineapple juice

5 fl oz (150 ml) dark rum

Planter's punch, a popular drink throughout the Caribbean, is a delicious combination of rum, orange, lime and pineapple juice, with just a trace of cinnamon and nutmeg. The syrup for this fruit salad is based on exactly the same combination, which makes it very special indeed.

Begin by making up the syrup: put the sugar, cinnamon sticks and 10 fl oz (275 ml) water in a small saucepan, then add the lime zest. Now, over a gentle flame, heat slowly until all the sugar has dissolved – it will take about 10 minutes. Stir it with a wooden spoon: you should have no sugar crystals left clinging to the spoon when you turn it over. After that, remove it from the heat and allow it to cool.

Add the prepared fruit to a large serving bowl, scooping the seeds from the halved passion fruit, using a teaspoon, then strain in the cold syrup, along with the fruit juices, lime juice and rum. Stir well before covering with clingfilm and chilling in the fridge. As you serve the fruit salad, sprinkle a little freshly grated nutmeg over each serving.

Eton Mess

Serves 6

6 oz (175 g) golden caster sugar

3 large egg whites

1 lb (450 g) fresh strawberries, hulled

1 rounded tablespoon icing sugar, preferably unrefined

10 fl oz (275 ml) double cream

You will also need a baking tray, 11 x 16 inches (28 x 40 cm), lined with baking parchment.

Pre-heat the oven to gas mark 2, 300°F (150°C).

This recipe, inspired by the strawberry and cream dessert traditionally served at Eton College on the 4th of June, is great for nervous meringue makers – because the meringues are broken up it simply doesn't matter if they weep, crack or collapse. So you can practise making them over and over with this dish until you get them perfect and, at the same time, enjoy this amazingly good summer dessert. Don't forget, though, to make the meringues the day before you want to serve the pudding.

First, have the caster sugar measured out ready, then place the egg whites in a scrupulously clean bowl and whisk until they form soft peaks that slightly tip over when you lift the whisk. Next, add the caster sugar, about a tablespoon at a time, and continue to whisk until each tablespoon of sugar has been thoroughly whisked in. Now simply take rounded dessertspoonfuls of the mixture and place them in rows on the lined baking tray. Place the baking tray in the oven on the centre shelf, turn the heat down to gas mark 1, 275°F (140°C) and leave the meringues there for 1 hour. After that, turn the oven off and leave the meringues in the oven to dry out overnight, or until the oven is completely cold.

When you're ready to make the pudding, chop half the strawberries and place them in a blender, together with the icing sugar. Whiz the whole lot to a purée, then pass it through a nylon sieve to remove the seeds. Now chop the rest of the strawberries and whip up the double cream to the floppy stage.

All the above can be done in advance, but when you are ready to serve, break up the meringues into roughly 1 inch (2.5 cm) pieces, place them in a large mixing bowl, add the chopped strawberries, then fold the cream in and around them. After that, gently fold in all but about 2 tablespoons of the purée to give a marbled effect. Finally, pile the whole lot into a serving dish, spoon the rest of the purée over the surface and serve as soon as possible.

Conversions for Australia and New Zealand

Measurements in this book refer to British standard imperial and metric measurements.

The standard UK teaspoon measure is 5 ml, the dessertspoon is 10 ml and the tablespoon measure is 15 ml. In Australia, the standard tablespoon is 20 ml.

UK large eggs weigh 63-73 g.

Converting standard cups to imperial and metric weights

Ingredients	Imperial/metric
almonds, ground	6½ oz/185 g
almonds, whole/chopped	5 oz/150 g
apricots, dried, whole	6 oz/175 g
blueberries, fresh	5 oz/150 g
breadcrumbs, fresh	3 oz/75 g
butter	9 oz/250 g
cornflour	4½ oz/125 g
currants	5 oz/150 g
dates, pitted, chopped	6½ oz/185 g
flour, plain	4½ oz/125 g
flour, self-raising	4½ oz/125 g
flour, wholemeal	5 oz/150 g
hazelnuts, chopped	4½ oz/125 g
lard	9 oz/250 g
pecans, chopped	4½ oz/125 g
pumpkin, cubed	5 oz/150 g
raisins	4½ oz/125 g
raspberries, whole	4½ oz/125 g
rhubarb, chopped	4½ oz/125 g
rice, Arborio, uncooked	8 oz/225 g
semolina	4½ oz/125 g
strawberries, sliced/whole	5 oz/150 g
sugar, brown, soft*/ demerara	8 oz/225 g
sugar, granulated/caster	9 oz/250 g
sugar, icing	4½ oz/125 g
sultanas	4½ oz/125 g
treacle/molasses/syrup	12 oz/350 g

* Firmly packed

Liquid cup conversions

Imperial	Metric	Cups
1 fl oz	25 ml	⅛ cup
2 fl oz	55 ml	¼ cup
2¾ fl oz	70 ml	⅓ cup
4 fl oz	120 ml	½ cup
6 fl oz	175 ml	¾ cup
8 fl oz	225 ml	1 cup
10 fl oz	275 ml	1¼ cups
12 fl oz	340 ml	1½ cups
16 fl oz	450 ml	2 cups
1 pint	570 ml	2½ cups
24 fl oz	680 ml	3 cups
32 fl oz	1 litre	4 cups

A few ingredient names

bicarbonate of soda
baking soda

Bramley cooking apples
if unavailable, use green cooking apples

buttermilk
if unavailable, use ordinary milk

Cox's/Golden Delicious apples
if unavailable, use small/medium dessert apples

curd cheese
if unavailable, use cream cheese

double/whipping cream
thick cream

fromage frais
fromage blanc

golden caster/ granulated/icing sugar
if unavailable, use regular caster/ granulated/icing sugar

Grape-Nuts
if unavailable, use toasted, chopped nuts

ground almonds
almond meal

pudding rice
if unavailable, use Arborio rice

vanilla pod
vanilla bean

Index

Miki Duisterhof 6, 9, 11, 12, 19, 23, 27, 33, 34, 41, 45, 47, 55, 56, 60, 67, 70, 81, 85, 87, 90, 100, 103, 104, 119, 120, 124, 127, 128, 131

Peter Knab 15, 20/21, 24, 37, 61, 73, 74, 112, 116

JP Masclet 137

David Munns 16

James Murphy 64

Debbie Patterson 89

Michael Paul 6, 16, 31, 34, 42, 45, 48, 51, 52/53, 59, 60, 68, 70, 77, 78/79, 85, 93, 94/95, 99, 100, 107, 108, 116/117, 123, 133

Simon Smith 40, 123

Petrina Tinslay 28, 82, 96, 100, 111

Delia Smith is Britain's best-selling cookery author, whose books have sold over 18 million copies. Delia's other books include *How To Cook Books One*, *Two* and *Three*, *The Delia Collection*: *Soup*, *Chicken*, *Fish*, *Italian*, *Pork*, *Chocolate* and *Baking*, her *Vegetarian Collection*, the *Complete Illustrated Cookery Course*, *One Is Fun*, the *Summer* and *Winter Collections* and *Christmas*. She has launched her own website. She is also a director of Norwich City Football Club, where she is in charge of Canary Catering, several restaurants and a regular series of food and wine workshops.

She is married to the writer and editor Michael Wynn Jones and they live in Suffolk.

For more information on Delia's restaurant,
food and wine workshops and events, contact:
Delia's Canary Catering, Norwich City Football Club plc, Carrow Road,
Norwich NR1 1JE; www.deliascanarycatering.co.uk
For Delia's Canary Catering (conferencing and events enquiries),
telephone 01603 218704
For Delia's Restaurant and Bar (reservations),
telephone 01603 218705

Visit Delia's website at www.deliaonline.com